THE
BERENSTAINS'
BABY BOOK

THE BERENSTAINS' BABY BOOK

BY STAN & JAN BERENSTAIN

PUBLISHED BY POCKET BOOKS NEW YORK

POCKET BOOKS, a division of Simon & Schuster, Inc.
1230 Avenue of the Americas, New York, N.Y. 10020

Published by arrangement with Arbor House Publishing Company
Library of Congress Catalog Card Number: 83-70467

ISBN: 0-671-49629-8

First Pocket Books printing July, 1984

10 9 8 7 6 5 4 3 2 1

POCKET and colophon are registered trademarks
of Simon & Schuster, Inc.

Printed in the U.S.A.

For Leo and Michael

Contents

1
Pregnancy

The most important thing to remember about pregnancy is that it's a perfectly normal condition. At first, you'll hardly know you are pregnant except during those brief and precious periods when something deep within reminds you that momentous changes are taking place.

Your first parental duty is to find a good doctor. Since compatibility between obstetrician and patient is absolutely essential, it is vital that you find an obstetrician who suits your personality and temperament. The following catalog of typical obstetricians may help you in considering your choice.

The Old Family Doctor
Old Doc Beamish has delivered 6,796 babies, including a fair number of his present patients.

The Taskmaster
Some women, lacking confidence in their own resources, prefer a
strict disciplinarian.

VIP (Very Important Physician)
Doctor to the international set. Merely to be on Dr. Miklemuch's patient list is a distinction. He has delivered personages of note all over the world, and may, at any minute, be called to attend a movie star, an heiress or a member of royalty—leaving an assistant you've never met to take care of you.

The Woman Obstetrician
Many women feel the female obstetrician, being a woman herself, will have a more sympathetic understanding of the patient's plight.

Before long, you will enter upon a regular obstetrical program. At first, you may find your experiences a little strange—even a bit bizarre.

But as you become adjusted to the routine of regular visits you will come to enjoy the camaraderie of the obstetrician's waiting room.

You may decide to investigate the "natural" childbirth method. This approach is based on the idea that full knowledge of birth as a natural process will banish fear and anxiety . . .

. . . and since fear and anxiety can be contagious, the husband as well as the wife must be fully indoctrinated.

Even when you reach the extreme late stages, your pregnancy is not a "confinement" in the Victorian sense. Of course, there are some things you'll do well to avoid . . .

. . . certain types of chairs,

. . . certain kinds of cars

MATERNITY EXPRESS

. . . and sudden starts and stops.

While you've been working through the final stages of your blimp impersonation, solicitous friends and relatives have kept your phone ringing off the wall. Your mother-in-law is convinced that the whole process is taking much too long and that your delaying tactics are for the specific purpose of embarrassing her.

Your fancy obstetrician calculated the date on which you are to be become a parent, has circumscribed a four-week period as a general target area and, at its chronological center, pinpointed the natal day. But now that you are well into the *succeeding* four-week period, it becomes clear that, like Truman in '48, you are going to make monkeys out of the experts.

At long last, however, you detect the unmistakable signs and portents and, after a mad dash, you arrive at the hospital sixteen hours early.

A NAME FOR BABY

BOYS

Name	Meaning
Amos	Industrious, serious, dues-paying
Andy	Lazy, silly, non-dues-paying
Anthony	See Antony
Antony	Seeing Cleopatra
Barney	Googly-eyed
Basil	Wrathful, boney
Ben	Short for Benjamin
Benjamin	Long for Ben
Bob	No, I'm Ray
Donald	Loquacious, incomprehensible, web-footed
Egbert	He's your kid, lady
Ernest	Frank
Ethelbert	Scarred for life
Frederick	Corruption of Fredryck
Horatio	Proud of his bridgework
Ken	Enamored of Barbie
Llewellyn	Diminutive of Lllewelllyn (Wellsh)
Orville	Wrighteous
Otto	Reverse spelling of Otto
Owen	In debt
Ron	Hewer of wood, getter of votes
Roswald	He'll hate you
Rudolph	Red-nosed
Siegfried	We dare you
Thomas	Hardy
Wilbur	Flighty

GIRLS

Name	Meaning
Adeline	Sweet
Amy	Little woman (also: Beth, Jo and Meg)
Antoinette	Scatterbrained
Barbie	Hot for Ken
Barbra	Adenoidal
Brunnhilde	Fat
Cloë	Much sought after
Delilah	Snippy
Esmeralda	Wonderful! A baby sister for little Roswald
Evita	Musical
Gail	Windy
Gaiyle	No such name
Isabella	Gullible
Isolde	Very fat
Jane	Mate of Tarzan
Jill	Fetcher of water
Katrina	Chases dirt (Old Dutch)
Mae	Inexcusable spelling of May
Shirley	Friend of Laverne
Susan	Lazy
Susanne	Very lazy
Sylvia	Enigmatic

2
Helpers—and Others

After about seventy-two hours of fitful bed rest and a few hours of gingerly interaction with your issue, you are evicted from the hospital, the tired but trim mother of a superlative little baby. Mother, Father and Baby are now on their own, a proud little family unit— and they should insist on remaining so until they have had a chance to set up their defenses. In nearly all cases it is a fatal mistake to accept offers of help from the maternal grandmother. The paternal grandmother, of course, is absolutely out of the question.

The fact is that there is nothing particularly difficult about caring for a brand-new baby. An infant's daily needs are extremely simple: food, dry clothes, a bath and sleep. The new baby will sleep as much as twenty hours a day, as though instinctively determined to make the most of this antisocial luxury while it's possible. Though the new mother is usually perfectly able to care for her baby, she is under doctor's orders to forego general household duties. As an interim factotum, Daddy is her best bet. The shiny new Daddy is obedient, dedicated, even worshipful, and makes the ideal postnatal auxiliary engine; also, he's had about nine months to wangle a week's leave from his job—two, if he's any kind of operator.

Don't interpret the fact that your newborn may sleep as much as twenty hours a day to mean you will be able to catch up on your reading. It will take you at least that long to contend with your mail, your phone and your doorbell. It seems, dear parent, that you have joined a list. Privy to this list are all the manufacturers, salesmen, entrepreneurs, promoters and con men whose commodities have remotely to do with babies, and it turns out that they are all fanatically interested in your new status as a parent. Every mail brings a slew of letters offering sincerest congratulations and multitudinous marvels designed to take the sting out of parenthood—a whole line of indispensables ranging from bibs to bar rags, a miraculous combination feeding chair/play table/toilet, a charter membership in the Toy-of-the-Month Club and a fascinating brochure on a revolutionary new method of birth control based somehow on the international date line.

You will be reminded that it is not your child's exclusive function to come trailing clouds of glory: about every fifth phone call will be put through by the representative of a wide-awake diaper service soliciting your baby's business. The caller will be a smiley-voiced young lady who seems not to hear your statement to the effect that you are already committed to disposable diapers, and is still in there pitching when you hang up.

Members of the AHNP (the Association for the Harassment of New Parents) are not above using the direct approach. Even before Mommy has lost her hospital legs, there will come a knocking at your chamber door. "How do you do, sir?" (Answering the door is one of Daddy's jobs.) "May I take the liberty of congratulating you on the birth of your new baby? I represent the Dawn Studios, specialists in baby photos. We are prepared to . . ." Members of the AHNP are specifically excepted from protection under the assault laws.

Your duties as secretary, receptionist and switchboard operator will make it difficult for you to get to know your youngster during the day, but don't despair. Baby's nocturnal activities will enable you to get pretty well acquainted during the wee hours.

Your friends and relatives will form a little club of their own, and, unfortunately, to these well-wishers you are obliged to be reasonably polite. The first meeting of the association will be held at your house, preferably in the nursery, and the chief topic for discussion will be the baby's resemblance to one or the other of its parents. Thank them all for the lovely presents, appoint yourself sergeant at arms and adjourn the meeting just as soon as a majority opinion has been reached.

One of the parent's most arduous duties is the protection of the child from doting grandparents. The road to spoiled children is paved with grandparents' good intentions. The situation is particularly dangerous if your baby is the first grandchild, but not until the tenth or so can you afford to ignore the hazard.

The situation is an even more unholy mess if all four grandparents reside in the same city. The visits then become a mad competition between in-laws. Following are listed some of the subversive activities engaged in by grandparents, together with appropriate countermeasures which you should take:

1. The grandparent's first impulse upon seeing the grandchild is to pick him up. It matters not that the child is happy in the crib, coach or playpen. Nor does it matter that it required a supreme effort of stamina, will and native cunning to get him to lie there quietly in the first place. *Up* he's snatched! Then, after a few minutes of knee dandling, Grandpa glances at his watch and discovers that he'd better hurry if he's going to pick up Grandma in time to make the first show. After all, he just

dropped in for a few minutes, and doesn't want to keep you folks. So, putting Baby back where he found him, he bids you adieu; but you don't hear him over the mounting decibels from your infant.

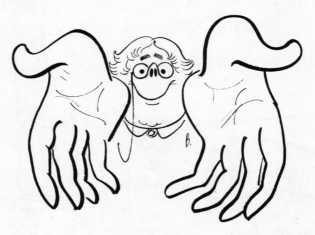

In this matter, as in all dealings with grandparents, *be firm.* Make it perfectly clear that it is *your* baby and is *not* to be picked up without your permission. Hurt feelings may result, but that can't be helped. Remain deaf to the argument that they managed to bring *you* up all right; the only rebuttal to that is unflattering to yourself.

2. Grandparents will feel it is their right to drop in without warning at any time of the day or night. If these impromptu visitations are permitted, you will soon be bordering on gibbering idiocy. Far better to have an early understanding on the subject than to let the pressure mount until you explode. If you are nursing your baby (and this is an excellent reason for doing so), you can modestly insist that Baby dine unattended. Since they are not interested in sleeping infants, that cuts out several more hours of the day which would be convenient for visiting. Point out that their grandchild's regular schedule is what's responsible for the weight gains and general well-being, and if they approve of such good health it follows that they must approve of the schedule. Give them a place on the schedule; if

it interferes with a lodge meeting or an appointment at the hairdresser's, so be it.

3. "Bearing gifts, they traverse afar": in this sense only do most grandparents resemble wise men. Every visit, scheduled or unscheduled, is complicated by what comes with it. Candies, cookies, outsize stuffed animals and wind-up toys which can be operated only by an adult are their stock-in-trade. Within a matter of minutes the candies and cookies are distributed about the floor, the nightmarish pink horse is permanently established in Daddy's easy chair and "Leaping Lena"—a miniature replica

of a circus jalopy—careens wildly around the room until it rams a fragile table supporting an equally fragile electric clock. Neither Lena nor the clock ever runs very successfully thereafter.

The happiest way to deal with this sort of thing is to gather up those toys which are not suitable and store them away as reserve. (The four-by-four pink horse you can leave out in the rain for a few days, and that will be the end of that.) As for the candies and cookies, *you* eat them.

4. Grandparents, as baby-sitters, are excruciatingly eager to please—the baby. But they *are* inexpensive. If you don't have to call on them too often to act in this capacity, you may be able to tell yourself, "Oh, what the hell," and enjoy the movie in spite of what you know is going on at home.

You may decide that the better part of valor is to hire a professional. Compatibility is important. Fortunately, there's a range of types.

Take-Charge Gal

"Now hear this!! While I'm sittin' I want it clearly understood who's in charge—and I don't take no stuff or no guff from nobody—kid or parent! . . ."

Experienced
"Oh yeah, Missus, I done all kinds of work—practical nursin', rivetin',
hash slingin', mangle operatin' . . ."

The Character
"I'm allergic to cats, dogs, house
dust, feather pillows, mohair and
chiming clocks. I require prune juice
and jasmine tea. About phone calls . . ."

The Perfectionist
"You'll notice I'm wearing what is known as a surgical mask. I have brought with me a supply of these . . ."

The Queen
"Hey, look. This is the third day this week you got home late!! Cream and sugar, please . . ."

The Surprise Package
"My sister couldn't come . . ."

If you are fortunate enough to find a dependable, nonexorbitant sitter, treasure her, coddle her, ply her with Arpege—*and* keep her name and phone number a dark secret from your less fortunate friends.

3

Feeding Time

"Gesundheit!"

Keep mealtime a pleasant, happy experience to which your child looks forward. Of course, your own enthusiasm for the ritual may be somewhat dimmed owing to the fact that the only food Baby seems to want is what's in the cat's dish under the sink. But don't give in. Though you have your work cut out for you, the task is not impossible. The key to success lies in your own attitude. If each meal is regarded as a contest, the parent will be the loser. It is impossible to reason a child into eating; the trick is to get the food into the baby without using force. Or, at least, without having to resort to a crowbar and a ramrod.

While there are many available generalizations on such feeding-time subjects as weaning, when and how to introduce solid foods, etc., they are not much help in dealing with your particular little General.

Accomplishing such steps as milk from the cup, finger food and utensils is largely a matter of trial and error—and error, and error and error.

You may start milk from the cup when Baby is as young as four or five months . . .

. . . or you may wish to wait until Baby is a little older and has greater lip and tongue control.

But whether you introduce the cup early or late, it's important to follow Baby's lead.

Different children react to solid food in different ways. Yours may be utterly bewildered by the first experience with solid food and reject it completely . . .

. . . or may take to it like a true little omnivore.

Yours will probably fall into the middle category of infants who can take solid food or leave it (taking what they like, of course, and leaving what they do not, even as you and I). You'll learn all those little preferences soon enough.

Your child may, for example, dislike spinach and other "strong" vegetables intensely, whereas the attitude toward cereal and starches may be one of bored intolerance . . .

. . . while at the "high interest" end of the preference pattern, Baby may be wildly enthusiastic about mashed banana or other dessert foods.

But since you have at least a moral obligation to feed a nutritious and balanced diet, you're going to have to find a way to get some of those nonpreferred foods past those locked jaws. Here is an approach that may work wonders.

As you sit down to feed your little impassive resister, pretend you are facing an adult dinner guest whose company you find delightful. Bring into play all the qualities which have won you a reputation as a charming hostess. If your table talk is sufficiently diverting, your child will never notice that the main course is strained liver. Discuss only subjects of mutual interest—the dog's latest trick, the cute little chipmunk that lives out back in Daddy's woodpile or the mole on the end of the nose of the lady next door, a subject that was abruptly opened for discussion in her presence only yesterday.

An important experience like a trip to the zoo can provide enough conversational ammunition to last you a half-dozen meals. Your little raconteur may have to disgorge a few mouthsful of mashed ripe banana in order to roar like a lion or bark like a seal, but the food ingested will substantially outweigh what is splattered on the wall. At subsequent meals Baby can eat beans like a rhino, chicken like a giraffe and noodles like a hippo. When it gets to the point of eating carrots like a two-toed sloth, you had better think up a new ploy.

Even the most pleasant meal will be peppered with mishaps. You must take these in your stride. You wouldn't embarrass an adult guest by showing annoyance when he knocks over his water glass; by the same token, you must ignore the warm milk trickling down your jeans. Continue reading *Little Willy Wombat* as though nothing had happened. So far, Little Willy has been good for seven spoons of baked potato, and may be worth seven more if you don't break the spell.

As Baby comes to feel more at home in the mealtime environment, he or she may develop little mealtime idiosyncrasies. Baby may decide simply that the meal isn't worth eating without a certain special spoon, for example.

But with the increase of neuromuscular control, Baby will develop new eating skills . . .

. . . will become an efficient chewer . . .

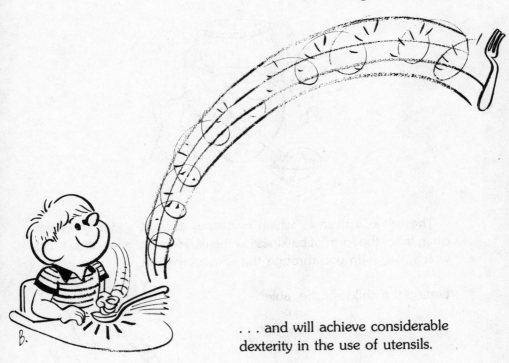

. . . and will achieve considerable dexterity in the use of utensils.

As personality develops, Baby's mealtime mood is bound to vary somewhat from meal to meal. If, however, your offspring's eating behavior seems to be going steadily downhill, it may be necessary to revaluate the mealtime climate. If a change of pace seems called for, Daddy might take over feeding for a while. Everything is a little more fun with Daddy.

The self-assertiveness which evidences itself at about age three often takes the form of balkiness at meals. Here are a few little tricks which may help you through this difficult period.

Letting the child set the table . . .

... select the menu ...

... or even help in the actual preparation of food.

You may find that a change of scene may do wonders for a lagging appetite—a luncheon party in his own room for his own toys using his own little table and chairs and cups and saucers, for example. Simply moving the mealtime outdoors may lend just the needed air of excitement.

Or you might ask your youngster's opinion about what might be a "fun" place to have lunch.

As you work with your youngster, his or her feeding "personality" will become readily apparent—and whether Baby turns out to be a "picky" eater, a two-fisted trencherman or something in between really doesn't matter as long as you and your pediatrician are comfortable with his weight-gain pattern and general health.

4
Bathtime

Once home from the hospital, a parent's first big task will be to give the newborn a bath. Though you had been anticipating this operation with considerable apprehension, a demonstration given by that redheaded snip of a nurse—during which she bathed a half-dozen assorted babies without even mussing her bangs—has almost convinced you there is nothing to it.

Having prepared your baby's "bath tray," a pink or blue waterproof affair that usually leaks, check the necessary items once again: boric acid, baby oil, baby cream, baby powder, castile soap, zinc ointment, Vaseline, absorbent cotton, swabs, tissues, comb, brush, nail clippers, safety pins and a strong sedative. Chuck that other stuff out: the gilt-initialed nail buffer (a shower gift which you thought "too cute for words" at the time), the angora powder puff with a silver safety pin for a handle (another shower gift) and the miniature

45

baby bottle filled with infant suntan lotion that squirts out through a miniature nipple (something for which you have only yourself to blame).

First a briefing on the operation of the bathinette. Some woolly-minded relative has probably given you the latest, most deluxe model: "You'll never use all the attachments, but they're nice to have." Well, they're not nice to have. Get rid of them. Strip the thing down until nothing remains but the bath hammock itself. One of the thousand gadgets you will remove is the draining hose. This will leave a hole in the bottom of the tub, which can be plugged with a bit of eraser from the end of a pencil. Although a bucket is needed to bail out the water at the completion of the bath, you have elimi-

nated the daily floods which would be the direct result of using the drainage hose. Some other attachments to be dispensed with are the all-too-collapsible Handi-Gadget Rack, the Handi-Spray (a hose arrangement ideally designed for fighting forest fires) and the handiest item of all—the Handi-Dressing Table, a canvas affair which will turn on you if not disposed of at the outset.

Now that you have seen to it that your equipment is in perfect working condition, partially fill the bath hammock with lukewarm water. Test it with your elbow. If you don't feel anything, it is just right. On the kitchen table to the left of the bathinette, undress Baby and cover the squirming body with a small towel. This serves to muffle screams, too. Swab the eyes, ears and nostrils with boric acid. Except for the face, on which you use water only, soap the baby thoroughly section by section, being especially careful to keep your youngster's soapy hands away from the face. Now lift the small towel, with Baby inside, and dunk the whole business in the bathinette. This will be like dunking a roaring outboard motor in a lily pond. Quickly return bathee to the table. Blot—don't rub—the baby dry; you can attend to yourself later. Sprinkle with baby powder, add diaper and clothes, and wade to the bedroom for a feeding. Suggest to Daddy that he put down that paper and at least clean up the kitchen before you institute divorce proceedings.

As children grow older they enjoy the bath more and more, and instead of crying when you put them in, they shriek indignantly when you take them out. At three months Baby will be flailing and thrashing like a hooked trout. At six months your tot will turn the bath water into a little piece of the English Channel with an excellent impersonation of Gertrude Ederle. At nine months, with the addition of an overall lurching and heaving motion, the bathinette will begin to travel precariously across the room, sloshing as it goes. At this point the contraption has outlived its usefulness. Collapse and store it, provided its last voyage did not reduce it to scrap. It has no trade-in value.

Introducing your nine-month-old to the "big" tub will be just that and nothing more for the first day. Your youngster will have no part

of it. Explaining that "that's where Mommy takes a bath, and Daddy, too," won't change anything. You may try the terribly modern approach of getting undressed and demonstrating *how* Mommy takes a bath in the big tub, but Baby will remain adamant. The kid's probably tired of being pushed around. No sooner had he developed a good steady drag on a bottle of milk than it was replaced with a cup; no sooner had he acquired the ability to sit than he was obliged to stand; and no sooner has he perfected the technique of navigating his bathinette than he is confronted with this large, cold and obviously unwieldy affair.

In the child's own good time, however, even the most stubborn will accept the new outrage. When you call to Daddy to come see his little doll taking a bath in the big tub, be sure to tell him to dress accordingly. Doll, in the meantime, has flung the plastic duck overboard, taken a few seal-like flips, manipulated the drain handle and, incredibly enough, yanked the chrome stopper out by the roots. For succeeding baths, it would be wise to have on hand a variety of seaworthy trinkets, beguiling enough to forestall the complete demolition of the plumbing accessories. Little boats, plastic or tin cups, celluloid fish or frogs (though Baby would be enchanted with the genuine articles), a dipper, a funnel, an ear syringe and a number of small balloons would be a good beginning. For the next few years these things will see the two of you through many a jolly aquacade. And it's obligatory: after all, you want to keep your angel at least within shouting distance of godliness.

5
Bedtime

Putting a really young child to bed is not normally a big problem—a full belly, a warm bed and your reassuring presence will usually do it. But putting an older bundle to bed is one of the severest drains on the wellsprings of intelligent parenthood. If you are to keep bedtime from resulting in the complete breakdown of discipline, you must formulate a plan for abetting the sandman before your child is old enough to see through your transparent schemes. Provided a sound bedtime routine is arrived at early in the game, Baby will have become so conditioned to bedding down by the time he starts feeling his oats that, although your tot's best efforts may drag the process out, they won't quite be able to drag it down.

A Regular Hour

Be just as insistent that your child goes to bed at a regular hour as your child is that you rise at a regular hour. If you are not firm on this point, you may as well turn in your uniform now.

Division of Labor

There is nothing in the Bible that says that putting to bed is woman's sole responsibility. With all that upper-body strength, Daddy is ideally suited for this back-breaking task. The important bedtime ritual usually begins with the nightly repetition of a favored game or activity. Children, being instinctively ritualistic, know intuitively that repetition is central to meaningful ritual . . .

. . . and insist upon perfect
execution of a rigidly
prescribed procedure . . .

. . . which leads inevitably to the moment of separation from
Mommy . . .

. . . and the crucial act
of going upstairs.

Going Upstairs
Going upstairs represents a symbolic break between the child and
the rest of the family, and can lead to serious separation anxiety if
badly handled.

   An exciting piggyback ride can provide a smooth transition.

Evening Bath
The evening bath is of great value in subduing your little valve-in-
head engine. Allow the child enough time to enjoy the evening tub,

but don't allow dawdling. A calm, quiet bath with some favored bath toys is a key event in the bedtime ritual.

After you've managed to get your tiny seal out of the tub and toweled off, allow the child to do the toothbrushing. Do the toothpaste squeezing yourself, of course, and use very little. Letting a small child get a grip on an open tube of toothpaste is sheer madness.

Bedtime Story

With the very young, the bedtime story should be a simple, somno-
lent narrative with no complex overtones. Your child will, almost
immediately upon the installation of bedtime stories as a regular
feature, insist on taking complete charge of programming. The
younger the child, the more likely the feeling that repetition, rather
than variety, is the spice of life. It is not unusual for a child who is
one and a half to insist on "Beantalk" for as many as forty-five nights
in a row. Toward the end of a long run like this, Fee, fi, fo, fum! can
have powerful emetic properties, and it's up to Daddy to keep a stiff
upper digestive tract.

Though dual-purpose weapons are usually unsatisfactory, it is
possible to make a subsidiary use of the bedtime story when the child
begins to develop a moral sense. By this time Daddy will have long
since worn out his stockpile of traditional stories, and found it necessary to write his own stuff. The injection of a little propaganda of a
virtue-rewarded persuasion into these homespun masterpieces may
exert a wholesome influence—until, that is, the little one's critical
faculties also begin to develop and an immunity to sermonizing is
built up. There are a few weeks in between, though, when you can
get in a few homiletic licks.

In all bedtime stories, to the traditional "and they all lived happily
ever after," it would be wise to append the coming of nightfall and
the retirement of all major characters. This may seem a cheap trick,
but it is really only one more legitimate exercise of parental license.
Handled with taste, these sedative codas can achieve the stature of
a minor art form. For example: "And then Aladdin rubbed his lamp
again. When the Jinni appeared, Aladdin said to him: 'Jinni, I am
very tired. I wish you to bring me the finest bed in the whole kingdom.' And the Jinni said: 'O Master, the finest bed in the whole land
belongs to little Ned Nitey, who is this very moment falling asleep
in it. Surely you do not wish to disturb him.' So Aladdin told the Jinni
to get him the second-finest bed in the kingdom, and when it was
done, Aladdin climbed into it and fell fa-a-ast asleep."

If, perchance, you are tempted to play a little fast and loose with some portion of the bedtime ritual . . .

. . . say, by skipping some component of a treasured story . . .

DON'T—you will be dealt with summarily!

Finally your efforts to put the bundle to bed will be rewarded and punctuated by the last act of the bedtime ritual—the goodnight kiss . . . But don't count on it.

Occasionally, the child will feel the need to expand the bedtime ritual—to make it more meaningful—and the sensitive parent recognizes such an occasion and does his best to cooperate.

After which he gets to work on a little bedtime ritual of his own!

PROGRESS REPORT

Since one of the principal propositions of this book is that children need to be dealt with as individuals, it might be instructive to consider the highly varied results obtained in a series of standardized tests administered to a group of randomly chosen children.

Test I—PAPER FOLDING

Examiner demonstrates the folding procedure, offers subject paper, and says, in calm, confident manner, "Here, you try it."

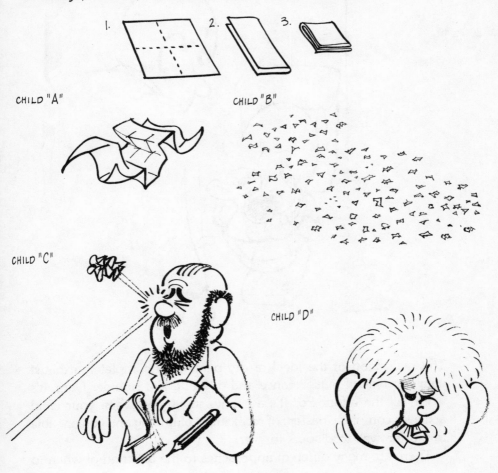

CHILD "A"

CHILD "B"

CHILD "C"

CHILD "D"

6
Toidy Days

The realization of the ideal of dry pants may completely exhaust your reserves of perseverance and grit, but, like Boulder Dam, it's worth all the effort. For it's a sunny, sunny day when your child achieves complete mastery of recalcitrant plumbing and you are able to bid farewell to diapers forever.

There are many different approaches to the question of when to start toilet training. The best approach in a particular case depends largely upon the individual "trainer." A relaxed parent who is inclined to take things in stride may prefer to wait for the problem to solve itself. Others may wish to begin toilet training early. If Baby is regular, early training may be simply a matter of noting the child's own rhythm and placing baby on the chamber at the same time each day.

On the other hand, a baby may be perfectly healthy and be very irregular.

This may make the toilet-training job a little more difficult, but you will soon learn to *sense* when to put Baby on the chamber—by a particular facial expression . . .

. . . or a favored stance.

Your own attitude toward the bathroom and its function is the key to your success. Throw all modesty out the window. Pocket the key to the bathroom door and keep the door open. Have a warm light glowing within, and toss a cozy mat upon the floor with the word WELCOME imprinted thereon. As soon as Baby is steeped in the jolly atmosphere of the place, and familiar with the role of the toilet in particular, it is time to set up your tot's own little throne.

However you approach the toilet-training problem, you will want to consider a toidy for Baby. There are two toidy alternatives.

You can get Baby a special toilet—it consists of a cabinet and a receptacle, with a seat on top. Besides being low and accessible to Baby, this type of arrangement offers the added convenience of being easily transportable from one part of the house to another.

Or you may prefer getting just the toidy seat. The separate unit with a detachable training seat is recommended. This seat may later be used on the big toilet. It should be equipped with a deflector—seat and deflector being, preferably, all of a piece. This type of seat is the most desirable for boys and girls alike, the point being that, like a Western saddle, it makes dismounting difficult; also, a girl's seat would greatly inconvenience small male guests. To illustrate: a young trainee of our acquaintance was most bewildered when, having been invited to sit on little Debbie's toidy seat on the big toilet, he urinated into the sink opposite.

There is no shortage of practical toidies, of the type described, available in baby furniture departments—and even less of a shortage of highly impractical ones: a ten-inch lifesaver with a Disney Duck quacking at the helm; a spidery affair of blue plastic which collapses into pocket size for convenience when traveling but is not so convenient when it comes to a hurried reconstruction; and the hard-to-resist super-deluxe upholstered leatherette number which plays "Please to put a penny in the old man's hat" when it is sat upon.

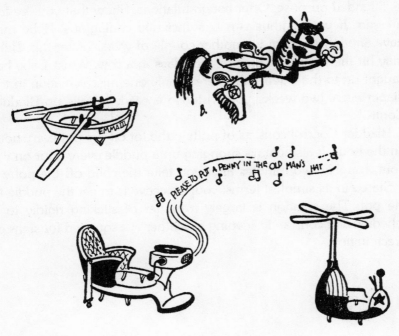

You may begin bowel training anytime after baby is able to sit up strongly. On the day you decide to take the plunge, wait until the time you usually expect a soiled diaper, then strap Baby on the new potty. Never refer to the strap as such, but by all means use it. Don't fasten it on the sly. After placing Baby in the seat, say simply, "I'll buckle your nice blue belt for you." Before those steely fingers begin testing it, stuff them with a banana, a piece of orange or some other intriguing food Baby's allowed to have but is seldom allowed to actually handle (for obvious reasons).

As the youngster sits there kneading a banana or massacring an orange, you must convey what it is that's expected. Your baby is too young to comprehend a long verbal briefing, but is apt to astound you with an ability to grasp the meaning behind a grimace or a grunt. If you are a particularly adept mime, your efforts may be rewarded the very first day. Don't be disappointed, though, if they are not. Actually, you have done well if all you have engendered in your trainee is a grimacing and grunting acceptance of the potty. Eventually, say in about two weeks, Baby may accidentally use the potty for its intended purpose. Offer congratulations. Show that you are impressed. If your enthusiasm is sufficiently contagious, Baby may have another accident in another couple of weeks. After this, Baby may hit the jackpotty three or four days in a row. When Baby has caught on to the extent that there is only one miscalculation in the diaper every two weeks, your virtuoso is ready to take up Bladder Control.

Bladder Control consists of putting the tot on the pot every hour on the hour. It also entails sponging up a puddle every hour on the hour, roughly two minutes after you take the child off the pot.

Stated in its simplest terms, your objective is to get the puddle in the pot. The solution is largely a matter of sticking rigidly to a schedule and constantly keeping a weather eye squinted for signs of precipitation.

Throughout the toilet-training program it is best to maintain a casual manner. When, however, Baby seems to catch on to the idea of the toidy, of course show that you are pleased.

On the other hand, if Baby doesn't immediately understand what is required, assume an attitude of patient understanding.

The time to dispense with the low chair and use the training seat on the big toilet comes when your toddler's legs grow long and sturdy enough to carry Baby, seat and all, into the next room to let you know he is "froo." You may try to strong-arm the underneath clamps into holding the seat to the chair more securely, but Little King Kong will be delighted by the challenge and drag the whole clanking business down the hall to help you see who's at the front door.

When your child graduates to the big toilet, appeal to pride by making it clear that it's a signal honor. It's the big league now, and unless Baby can keep up with the fast company, it'll be back to the minors for further seasoning.

Gradually, as Baby grows and gains confidence, he can be introduced to the big toilet and left pretty much to his own devices.

7

Illness

When your youngster shows signs of coming down with a cold, you may as well resign yourself to the proposition that you are going to take a licking. Your advantages in weight, height and reach compare favorably with those Goliath held over David, but you will be so hamstrung by doctor's orders that you are doomed to share the ultimate fate of your fellow Philistine.

You can hardly blame your invalid for setting up a howl as soon as the family physician comes into view. For all the chin-chucking, the doctor is just an extension of a hypodermic syringe to Baby, and the howling isn't likely to cease until Doc is on the way out.

If you hear yourself saying, "It won't hurt, sweetie!" bite your tongue. Always tell as much of the truth as your child can understand —if not out of a fundamental moral imperative, then at least in an effort to establish and maintain the most valuable attribute you have as a parent—your credibility. If you con your three-year-old into believing that the shot won't hurt, why should he or she believe your later claims that marijuana, booze and skipping school will?

Afterwards, you study the page of instructions you took down with one hand while rapidly undressing and dressing your screaming pinwheel with the other. As nearly as can be made out, your scribblings read as follows:

> kpchd inbd untl tmpisnm
> 1 tspnf prcn ev3hrs
> nsdps at bdtm if nc
> plty of lqds.

Don't get panicky. The key to this cryptogram is the telephone. Take a look at the prescription (thank heaven you don't have to read *it*), and note the office hours at the top. Then simply phone the office and review the directions. The good doctor will be expecting your call.

The fly in your healing ointment is the item "kpchd inbd untl tmpisnm," which has been translated to read, "Keep child in bed until temperature is normal." It would help no one to make public the intelligence that even the most expensive pediatricians are unable to carry out this mandate. Yours not to reason why, yours but to make an honest effort to keep your sniffle-machine in bed. The best you can hope for is to render Baby comparatively inactive for a while—say, for six consecutive minutes at a time.

The most effective method for keeping a small child quiet is dishearteningly like the most effective method for getting a small child to do anything he's agin: distraction. It is superfluous to point out that this is more easily said than done. By the time the average child is about two, the average parent has been squeezed dry of the ability to distract. The following list is for the benefit of these mummies and daddies who are beyond thinking up new ways of degrading themselves:

Songs

Dredge your subconscious. Perhaps you'll come up with "The Monkeys Have No Tails in Zamboango," "Way Down in Dear Old Borneo" or "I Can Dance with Everybody but My Wife." Try to recall your old school songs and yells. Properly bowdlerized Army and Navy songs may fascinate the convalescent into plucking at the coverlet for an extra hour.

Stories:

If your repertory is completely exhausted and you are too enfeebled to make up new ones, try scrambling the old ones. "Rumpelstiltskin and the Forty Thieves," "Ali Baba and the Seven Dwarfs" and "Snow White and the Beanstalk" have a certain shock value and may help to keep the invalid idling in neutral for another hour.

Parlor Tricks

Ear wiggling, knuckle cracking, the handkerchief cradle trick, the separating thumb illusion, the Here's-the-church-and-here's-the-steeple-open-the-doors-and-see-all-the-people routine are all sound, if admittedly demented.

"1 tspnf prcn ev3hrs" (one teaspoonful prescription every three hours). This is another catch-as-catch-can imbroglio. Your doctor knows as well as you do that baby simply won't down anything that doesn't taste pretty. As a consequence, you can trust Grimes Drugstore and Candy Kitchen to produce an elixir which will discourage the cold germs without offending their host's discriminating palate. It does not follow, of course, that the patient will permit a dosing without a fuss in any case. It is traditional that Mommy or Daddy join Baby every three hours in a therapeutic toast. Don't resent the spoonfuls of perfumed glue you are called upon to swallow in line of duty. The germs have heard about you, too, and like as not are infiltrating your own esophagus right now.

Decoded, "nsdps at bdtm if nc" reads, "Nose drops at bedtime if necessary." If your offspring is one of the vast majority who greets the sandman with thumb in mouth, you really have no choice but to resort to nose drops. The only alternative to clearing that stuffy little nose is to try to get Baby to shift to stogie-style thumb-sucking, breathing out of the other side of the mouth. Not many children can manage this, so drops are required. Administering them is a two-person job; and since it is of extreme importance that patient and curators get all the sleep they can, no holds are barred.

8
First Toys

Whether you are choosing a toy for a newly arrived bundle whose skills are confined to sucking and flailing, or a four-year-old home-maker who has expressed a fierce desire for a real stove, with a real oven, equipped with an automatic timer and a real pressure cooker suitable for canning, a high degree of critical judgment should be exercised.

When selecting toys for tiny babies, all other considerations must be ignored in favor of this paramount one: the child's safety. Make your decision on the basis of what may be called the toy's "suckability." This leaves out all the furry, cuddly, squeezy, jingly things well-meaning relatives and friends have sent, and, with the exception of those fetus-like rubber dollies and grotesque little plastic fish, practically everything in the toy store, too. There are available, to be sure, a few toys scientifically designed for infants. These are often especially commissioned by progressive toy companies from famous industrial designers and carry a snappy price tag. But for parents of ingenuity, there is a way out. For in any American five-and-ten, the same money will buy a whole battery of toys with superlative suckability ratings, provided, of course, you stay away from the toy counter. The pet department is a good place to start. A dog bone, Saint Bernard size, is an ideal infant's toy. It is made of an excellent grade of rubber, is practically indestructible, eminently washable and costs next to nothing. On your way to the houseware counter to get a set of brightly colored measuring spoons on a ring, stop by the hardware department and pick up the business end of a sink plunger; as Baby gets older, graduate to a larger size. There are literally dozens of blunt, colorful plastic and rubber items for sale in the five-and-ten which make excellent infant's playthings and have the added value of remaining useful after baby has outgrown them. There's no telling when an extra plunger may come in handy.

When your child is about six months old, it's time to start hauling out the stuff that has been arriving in a steady stream since you left the hospital, but which so far wasn't deemed quite suitable. Baby is now ready for the heady pleasures of stuffed animals. These should not be taken down from the closet shelf and presented en masse, but should be produced one at a time and applied when they will do the most good. This stockpile of giant pandas, fuzzy ducks, teddy bears and cuddly bunnies can prove a valuable strategic weapon during spells of colic, sieges of teething and in the breaking of hunger strikes. They should never be offered as a bribe or as a direct reward, but should be used for diversionary purposes.

Even the very young child will develop maniacal passions for certain playthings and will insist on taking a few of these very dearest friends along at bedtime. It's a bit lonesome in there all alone, and it's understandable to want the company of Pluto the dog, Ding-Dong the elephant, Fifi the French poodle, Piggy-Wiggy, Bunny-Bun-Bun and others too revolting to mention. Incredibly enough, Baby is perfectly able to get a good night's sleep in this menagerie. But if you'd rather not have your tot spend the night under conditions as congested as the stadium for a Superbowl game, it's safe to tiptoe in later and thin the ranks a bit. Just be sure you don't tuck in Raggedy Andy and consign Baby to the toy box with Pluto, Ding-Dong, Fi-Fi and the rest.

COMFY OBJECT AT 4 MONTHS

COMFY OBJECTS

Psychological research has shown the importance of the favored toy, or "comfy object." This is the special toy or object with which the child comes to identify, and which is necessary in times of transition, during trips away from home and while falling asleep at night.

A recent survey shows the following preferences for particular comfy objects:

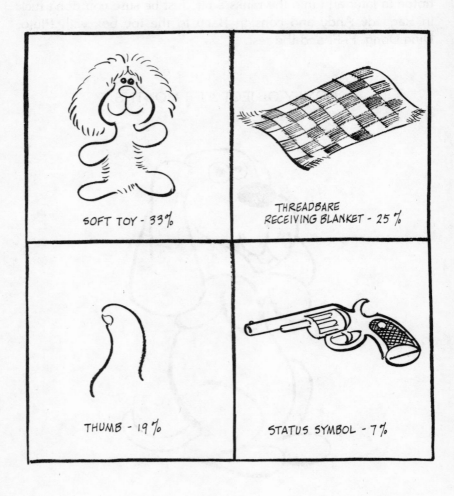

SOFT TOY - 33%

THREADBARE RECEIVING BLANKET - 25%

THUMB - 19%

STATUS SYMBOL - 7%

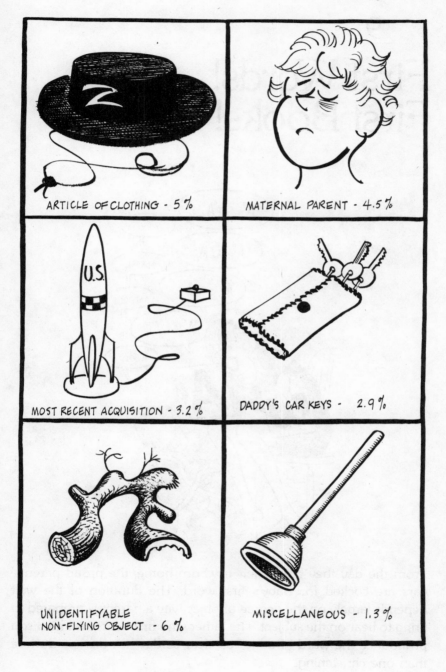

ARTICLE OF CLOTHING - 5%

MATERNAL PARENT - 4.5%

MOST RECENT ACQUISITION - 3.2%

DADDY'S CAR KEYS - 2.9%

UNIDENTIFYABLE
NON-FLYING OBJECT - 6%

MISCELLANEOUS - 1.3%

9

First Words!
First Books!

From the day they bring their newborn home, the proud parents' ears are cocked for Baby's first word. The duration of the wait depends largely on the degree of objectivity a parent is prepared to bring to bear on the subject. The father who first hears his infant son pronounce the word "Daddy" as clear as day has disrupted more than one christening.

It takes considerable restraint to keep from interpreting your small one's every gurgle as an addition to a rapidly expanding vocabulary; but to be brutally realistic about it, the very young baby is physically and mentally incapable of genuine speech. This is not to say that a three-month-old cannot say "da-da" or "ma-ma." Many of them do, but it is merely an unconscious reflex, a mechanical mouthing of those particular sounds. They say "ga-ga" and "la-la" with equal conviction.

When your baby is about eight months old, he or she will probably produce that magical first word. For our purposes here, a word is loosely defined as a specific sound with a specific meaning. For some reason, parents generally assume that Baby's first words will be "Ma-ma" and "Da-da." Perhaps they feel it's the least Baby can do to show some appreciation. Well, in most cases, they are sorely disappointed. Their child's first effort might be anything from the simple word "ball" to a garbled version of "Wisteria," the cat's name. Actually, your child's speech will for a long time consist not so much of words, but rather of highly questionable approximations of words. It might be helpful to indicate right now with fearless candor what your fifteen-month-old's vocabulary actually amounts to:

The actual word	*Your child's version*
ball	bah
shoe	ooh (very high-pitched, with puckered lips)
pillow	baba
umbrella	umbaba
I want	(two swine-like grunts)
toilet paper	bay-*pah!*
what's that?	zat?
water	lala
glass of water	googalala
trolley	baba
baby	bebe
bus	beh
banana	nanna
Grandmom	nanna
airplane	r-r-r-r-r!

There's nothing abnormal about this state of affairs; you'll get the hang of it before long, like African explorers coping with the native dialect. But at this point, a strong word of caution: *Do not indulge in the use of baby talk!* If you succumb to the temptation, which, granted, is great, your punishment will be swift and terrible. You will be saddled with umbaba, bay-*pah* and googalala for years to come. Besides, if you encourage the child by imitation, you are being grossly unfair: a small child is susceptible to flattery, and will treasure the baby talk which has earned such an appreciative audience. Baby will not be able to understand why words and expressions which were once so satisfactory become objectionable to the very people who once found them worth imitating. We're not saying the kid is heading for the psychiatrist's couch, but serious maladjustment can result from more trivial causes. Call a spade a spade, not a pade.

Once a child gets the hang of a particular word, don't be too surprised (or embarrassed) if you hear it used indiscriminately and to excess.

As they tune in to language, children just seem to naturally gravitate to vocabulary we'd rather they didn't acquire. Your first intimation that your little one has been sponging up all your oaths, epithets, asides and chance remarks about in-laws and neighbors can be one of life's most profoundly mortifying experiences. The time and place vary with the child, although invariably both are remarkably well chosen. A one-year-old can do the job as neatly as a two-year-old, making up in succinctness for any feebleness in vocabulary.

For instance, it will dawn on you that from now on you had better watch your words when your one-year-old utters a particular one in a crowded, acoustically perfect bus. What word, we won't say. (Goodness knows *where* your angel picked it up!)

As children grow older, their memories absorb like blotting paper and their sense of timing becomes more acute. Thus, the longer the child waits for just the right moment, the more exquisite the parent's torture is likely to be. Imagine lifting your three-year-old so that he or she can look into the baby carriage at Mrs. Dugan's new twins, and hearing, "Mommy *said* you looked like you were going to have twins."

As with any situation which sees you and your child at odds, you are basically helpless. This is not to say that you can afford to sit back and let poor enough alone, for, as with any situation which sees you and your child at odds, it can get immeasurably worse. The first thing to do is assess the damage. Since it was about two months ago that you made your passing remark about Mrs. Dugan's appearance, you are warned that anything you may have said during that time can be used against you. In other words, little Wotan is well stocked with thunderbolts.

The outlook, though fraught with peril, is not completely hopeless. In a general way you can prepare some defenses against your toddler's loose tongue. List mentally the people you are most likely to have slandered in recent months. List only the worst cases, people against whom you have conducted a running campaign of invective. On these, Baby has a complete dossier of items which won't bear repeating. Suppose you should suffer a visitation of The Plague—your pet name for sister-in-law Maxine. See to it that child and aunt are rigidly segregated. Some ordinarily forbidden treasure, such as Daddy's college yearbook, can be offered up in a sacrificial sort of way to distract Baby until the danger is past. Meanwhile, if you keep the conversation moving, and on a low enough plane, it won't occur to your guest to play the attentive aunt.

Of course, things can't always be handled so neatly. In most cases there isn't time for preparation. You'll often have to be able to manage a sudden and gargantuan sneeze to drown out the offending word or phrase. Sometimes a spontaneous peal of hysterical laughter is called for, or even a sharp scream. You will have to think fast to explain these curious demonstrations, but it can be done. If things get really grim, though, you may simply have to clap your hand over the little mouth.

An unexpected reprise of a causal verbal indiscretion is bad enough, but to have your child suddenly volunteer a highly unsuitable idiom can be much worse, especially if your most staid neighbor is calling to discuss your possible participation in the forthcoming neighborhood bazaar. To prevent this sort of disaster, the parent must take an inventory of personal language habits and resolve to discontinue the use of all profanity. Generally Daddy is the principal culprit in this respect. He no doubt needs a good bit of toning down, and Mother will have to be in charge of the project. The battle will be half won if she can somehow gear the thing to his pocketbook. This is the procedure to follow:

First, notify him that he must stop using such atrocious language. He will be astounded, and in all sincerity demand to know, "What atrocious language?" When he stops stewing, say pleasantly, "All right, then, if your language is so fit for young ears, perhaps you'll agree to a little experiment." Whereupon you whip out an agreement that reads something like this:

> In order to curb our use of objectionable language in the presence of our child, we, the undersigned, agree to the following schedule of penalties, said penalties to be forfeit to the other party to this agreement:

Objectionable slang	10 cents
Anatomical references	25 cents
Profanity (simple)	35 cents
Profanity (compounded)	50 cents
Obscenity	75 cents
Compound profanity and obscenity	One dollar

With his child's welfare at stake, Daddy can hardly refuse to sign the contract. Though he will have embarked on the venture in order to protect his child, it will be a desire to protect his pocketbook that will accomplish the cleanup; he will soon find that he cannot afford the luxury of salty speech. Mother's reward is twofold: she can take pride in a job well done, and she can buy herself a little something with the dimes, quarters, halves and dollars that will inevitably accumulate, iron resolutions notwithstanding.

Conversation within earshot of your youngster, having dwindled to such bland stuff, may be somewhat frustrating. To a certain extent, pig Latin, high school French and the spelling out of words will provide outlets for a little steam. But be careful not to overdo it, or your little eavesdropper is likely to relay to wealthy Uncle Ben the intelligence that you have called him an ompous-pay, *stupide* old s-l-o-b.

Just as they are fascinated by the spoken word, children are fascinated by the written word. The conscientious parent introduces the youngster to books as soon as possible.

The importance of exercising extreme care in choosing the books which your child will read and reread cannot be overemphasized. Lack of intelligent discrimination in this matter can be so discouraging that the child may never come to know the wonderful world of books. Here are some questions to ask yourself about any book you are considering for your child:

1. If the child hits you with it, will it hurt?
2. What will be the effect on the book if the child takes it into the bath and gives it a good scrubbing with Daddy's toothbrush? Finally (and of least importance), what will be the effect on Daddy?

3. If half the pages are ripped out and torn to shreds, will it affect the story line?

4. In the event that the child demands it be read over and over again for as much as an hour, will it produce nausea?

5. Is the volume small enough to be quickly and easily hidden in the event that you *have* been forced to read it over and over again for as much as an hour and it *has* produced nausea?

6. Is the type bold enough to be read through a thin layer of strained squash?

7. Will it fill a specific need? Is it exciting enough to distract the child while you spoon in the cereal, or is it sufficiently soporific to produce sleep after a wild day at the sandbox?

If the answers to these questions seem to be in the book's favor and the cost isn't much more than four or five dollars, it won't do much harm to buy it.

Once you've bought the book, catchily entitled *Cockie-Lockie Bakes Some Cookie-Lookies,* and taken it home, what then? Should you just hand it over and say, "Here's a dollar book I brung ya"?

Definitely not! Hold on to it. It's money in the bank. Keep it under wraps until, in the normal course of events, a crisis arises. Then say, in your most casual manner, "If you don't stop eating the leaves off Mommy's nice philodendron, I won't give you the pretty new book I bought you." If you manage just the proper tone, Baby will stop. Baby might even spit out the latest mouthful. You then have Baby —and philodendron pulp—in the palm of your hand.

Your cherub sits down beside you on the sofa, and you begin to read. *"One bright sunshiny day, Cockie-Lockie got up and said, 'Isn't this a bright sunshiny day! I think I'll bake some cookie-lookies!' "* As you struggle through to the end of the tale, your docile little lamb leaps from the sofa and heads for the playroom. And is back in a flash with a tall stack of all the books stashed away in there. The little darling nestles down beside you, face lit with a happy, anticipatory

smile. There's nothing for it but to take the top book off the pile and begin to read: *"One bright sunshiny day, Bunny-No-Good was hopping down the path. As he hopped, he passed seven naughty dandelions. 'Naughty Dandelions,' he said . . ."*

Later—much later—you go numb and it isn't so bad.

COMFY OBJECT AT 6 MONTHS

PROGRESS REPORT

Test II—BALL THROWING

Examiner demonstrates act of throwing ball, offers subject ball, departs and views behavior from behind one-way viewing glass.

CHILD "A"

CHILD "B"

CHILD "C"

CHILD "D"

10
Self-Reliance

The little girl who is provided with simple polo shirts and jumpers will quickly learn to dress herself, while the little doll who is fussed up daily in starched petticoats and frilly pinafores that fasten in the back will have a wretched time of it. Similarly, the boy who is simply and comfortably clothed in T-shirts and boxer pants will be slipping into them "all by hisself" by the time he's four, whereas Little Lord Fauntleroy will rip off those complicated buttons in a rage when his mother heckles him with: "Heavens, darling, try dressing yourself once in a while. A big four-year-old boy like you!"

At two and a half, your tot will probably try to remove socks by grabbing at the piggie end and pulling toward his face. He pulls and pulls. Nothing happens. Eventually his hand slips off and connects with his nose. After this, be sure to slip his socks off his heels for him when he's in the mood to undress himself. Then when he grabs a handful of sock and yanks, he'll get results: there will be a sock in his fist when it connects with his nose.

A few months later he'll catch on to the heel-first gimmick, and then attack the shoe-removing problem. First, he'll tug at the shoe-laces until they are securely knotted; then, after a long, hard pull, he'll clout himself smartly on the forehead when the knotted shoe finally leaves his foot.

In spite of the bumps and bruises on the outside, inwardly your child is bursting with pride. The "I do it myself!" stage has arrived. During this period every day is highlighted by an unaided attempt to perform a new feat. The degree of this daily disaster depends on the parent's ability at sleight of hand. If, between the time of the screeching decision, "I do it myself!" and the actual deed, Mommy is able to sidle into the bathroom, kick the step-up in place, lift the toilet seat and retire to a neutral corner without arousing suspicion, Baby will perform that first unassisted void with relative success.

You may expect your child to do the following things as the desire for independence is asserted:

AT 3 MONTHS YOUR CHILD . . .

. . . recognizes and responds to a human face . . .

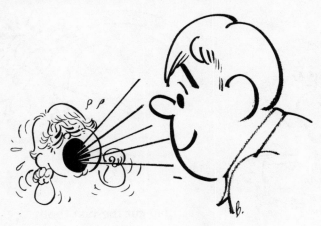

... fixes gaze on near object ...

... smiles in response to friendly overtures.

AT 6 MONTHS YOUR CHILD ...

... may recognize Daddy ...

... may cut the first tooth.

AT 9 MONTHS YOUR CHILD . . .

. . . may evidence an irrepressible urge to pull himself up to his feet.

Initial failure will just strengthen his resolve to try again . . .

. . . and, if need be, again . . .

. . . until he succeeds.

AT 12 MONTHS YOUR CHILD . . .

. . . makes tentative overtures to adults . . .

. . . may feed himself mashed potatoes—with his hands.

AT 18 MONTHS YOUR CHILD . . .

. . . loves to perform little errands . . .

. . . is enthusiastic about "clean up" activities.

AT 20 MONTHS YOUR CHILD . . .

. . . begins to feel a burgeoning sense of possession and property.

It's *his* pussy cat . . .

. . . *his* toidy.

AT 24 MONTHS YOUR CHILD . . .

. . . has much greater manual control than heretofore, and can—turn
pages . . .

. . . manage faucets . . .

. . . use scissors.

AT 36 MONTHS YOUR CHILD . . .

begins to have strong feelings of independence which are expressed in a fierce need to "do it myself." The child

. . . insists on tying his own shoes . . .

. . . squeezes his own toothpaste . . .

. . . is willing to undertake the job of undressing himself.

AT 4 YEARS YOUR CHILD . . .

. . . can dress himself—provided the complete attire consists of a cowboy hat and Daddy's slippers.

AT 5 TO 6 YEARS YOUR CHILD . . .

. . . can do everything which up to now he *thought* he was doing "all by myself."

PROGRESS REPORT

Test III—FORM BOARD

Examiner demonstrates Form Board, disassembles it, offers it to subject and says, encouragingly, "Here, you try it."

CHILD "A"

CHILD "B"

CHILD "C"

CHILD "D"

11

First Games

As a parent, you have an obligation to spend as much time as possible at play with your child. The sense of security, the self-confidence, the mental and physical exercise and the development of group spirit which these play sessions will encourage in your offspring are vastly important contributions to the child's general well-being.

Herewith some suggested games and activities for parents and kiddies:

1. Bom-Bom-*Bootz!:* You can begin playing this with your child as soon as the soft spot in the skull, just above the forehead, closes. Do not indulge in this game after your child reaches the age of two. There are reliable records of parents having suffered serious concussions from playing Bom-Bom-*Bootz* with overage youngsters. Queensberry rules: the parent crouches on the floor facing the child. (For parents, all games entail physical hardships.) In unison they cry, "Bom-Bom-*Bootz*!" and crash their foreheads together. Baby is delighted,

screams with hysterical laughter. Parent accepts two aspirins proffered by mate, who is scheduled to play the winner.

2. Peekaboo: This game is very popular with children between the ages of one and one and a half. It has the advantage of requiring no special equipment or talent, and the disadvantage of being utterly inane. To play, the parent must crouch down behind a chair or sofa on which Baby stands facing the back. Parent leaps up, grimaces wildly, and shouts, *"Peekaboo!"* Baby is delighted, screams with hysterical laughter. This routine is repeated until booee's knees give out or until booer falls exhausted to the broadloom.

3. Round-and-Round: This game occurs spontaneously to the children a few minutes after they learn to walk, and remains a

popular after-dinner activity until they are old enough to know better. It is fiendishly simple, consisting merely of both parent and child standing in the middle of a room and revolving, at first slowly, then more and more rapidly until the speed of an oriental dervish is achieved. Baby is delighted, screams with hysterical laughter. This is continued until, in the case of the parent, an overwhelming nausea sets in. Children seem to be able to keep it up indefinitely, but of course they smoke and drink less and get more sleep and eat next to nothing for dinner. That this is your little one's idea of fun, however, is pretty dismaying. Still, if Baby elects to play Round-and-Round, there's nothing for it but to pocket your editorial opinion and make like a pinwheel.

4. Hide-and-Seek: In your efforts to educate your small bundle of muscle to less homicidal forms of recreation, you mention Hide-and-Seek, a game remembered fondly by most parents. With great persuasiveness the rules of the game and its peculiar charms are described. No sale. Hide-and-Seek just isn't exciting and Baby expresses not the slightest interest in it—that is, not until a little later in the evening when the word "bedtime" is mentioned. Then little Houdini stages a disappearing act that needs only a flash of fire and a smell of sulphur to complete the effect. Finally, having searched high and low, you find the missing person—low—absorbing dust under Daddy's desk in the study. To your stern injunctions to come out of there and behave, you get a righteous protest: "I only playin' Hide-'n'-Seek!"

5. Horsey: This is a fine old traditional diversion which helps father and child get to know each other real well. It helps Dad to get better acquainted with himself, too, in that he is reintroduced to muscles with which he hasn't been on flexing terms for more than a decade. Pop's part in the game is brutally elementary: he pretends he's a horse. For his little playmate, the illusion is perfect, whatever private misgivings Horsey may entertain. With a bone-jarring leap the steed is mounted. "Giddap!" In an effort to coax more speed out of the sluggish nag, our rider digs sharp little heels into Horsey's tender flanks.

Horsey whinnies

in pain and gallops off around the coffee table. Baby is d. & screams with h. l. If these rodeos are allowed to become regular inclusions on the evening's agenda, Daddy's impersonations are apt to degenerate from prancing palomino to sway-backed, spavined glue bait.

There are other, and more bone-crushing, entertainments, but it is not the purpose of this book to be exhaustive. Your child will take care of that.

Until the toddler or, more accurately, "totterer," is about four years old, play periods with other youngsters will require adult supervision. Whether actual presence on the scene is necessary depends on the individuals at play, but being at all times within earshot and easy bounding distance is mandatory.

Let us look in on a simple game of building blocks. Leo—age two and a half—is strenuously erecting a wobbly column of blocks,

repeatedly intoning, "Dis is a big daddy hippo house wif a hippo pool in the back"; Debbie—age two—is squatting nearby with a block in each hand, sucking them alternately; and Carol—age three —is winging anything she can get her hands on at the cat under the crib.

Even as you enter the room unnoticed, a simple nonmalicious act of one child sets off a chain reaction of such blinding speed that you are unable to arrest it or even minimize its effects. Leo, having exhausted his supply of blocks, "borrows" one of Debbie's. Debbie hangs on for dear life, and bops him on the head with the block in her other hand, lodging a strong protest all the while. Carol, taking advantage of the fracas, wades into Leo's precarious hippo house, and the shattering crash diverts Leo's attack from Debbie. Possibly you will catch Leo in time to save Carol from a vicious frontal assault, but the ensuing tears, fury, hurt feelings and wounded pride are what require your major attention.

The two visitors are by now screaming, "I want my mommy!" and since the last thing you want is for their mothers to discover them in adversity under your roof, your first move is to the cupboard for lemon candies. With an uneasy truce thus won, philosophize with them. It is very important that however you preach the lesson to be learned from the incident, no one should be blamed for it. If it was anyone's fault, it was yours. Had you been on hand to direct Leo's attention to the unused blocks in the corner, he wouldn't have grabbed Debbie's. What you must do is take each in turn and point out what he or she did that made the others cry, and if possible, coax an apology from each. A box of unmedicated Band-Aids will effect a bit of magic at this point. When each has a patch over a real or imaginary bump, the misfortunes of war will be forgotten, and equanimity restored—at least, until someone decides to play with the only ball in the room alone.

The very small child doesn't care a fig about how nice it is to "share." If his Daddy gives him a ball, it's *his.* Everything in his room is *his.* Anything *anyone* has *ever* handed him is *his.* From the time he was an infant, no other person *ever* touched his personal treasures, for reasons of hygiene. By the same token, he wasn't permitted to handle other babies' toys. He was constantly being told, "No! No! That's Davey's rattle. Here's *your* rattle"; "No! No! That's Stevey's book. Here's *your* book!"

It's hardly surprising, then, that when confronted by an interloper, he guards his possessions with a ferocity that would do credit to a mountain lion. Before Debbie has a chance to wriggle out of her snowsuit, Leo gathers up an enormous number of things in his arms,

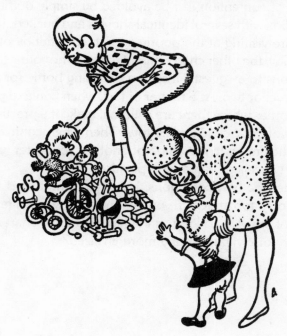

sits on as many others as he can, and exclaims: "Dis is mine! Don't you touch it! You can't have my bear! You can't have my duck! You can't have my cat! You can't have my Humpty Dumpty! Dis is *mine* toys!" A good way to resolve this dilemma is to demonstrate how profitable sharing can be. You should say, in a loud, judicial voice, "Well, now, it doesn't look like Debbie's going to have much fun sitting around doing nothing, so if Leo doesn't want her to play with his things, I'd be very happy to let her play with something of mine." As you hand Debbie your change purse with a couple of pennies in it, you say to bug-eyed Leo: "Now, Leo, don't you touch it! It's for Debbie to play with." Leo will then noisily abandon his loot, and his jaw will jut forward, signaling an impending cloudburst. Just as his lower lip begins to quiver, suggest, "Maybe Debbie will let you play with it, though, if you let her play with some of your nice toys." Debbie doesn't give a hoot about the purse (she's got one of her own at home full of quarters), but she would like to get her hands on Leo's bear, duck, cat and Humpty Dumpty, and yank their eyes out.

Many a tug of war in the sandbox with a shovel or bucket serving as the bone of contention can be avoided by simply outfitting your child's sandbox with several identical shovels and buckets. If you and your child are visiting at the poorly appointed sandbox of a neighbor, don't allow the other child's parent to force the youngster to give up possessions to a "guest." Insist on returning home for a supplementary shovel or two. As a matter of fact, when you and your child visit other homes where there are children, make it a practice to take along a few of your child's prize toys. Then when confronted with the don't-touch-mine toys routine of another youngster, your child will be in an excellent bargaining position.

Even under the best conditions, life among the tots is turbulent. So don't worry too much if your youngster's social life seems a succession of brawls—as long as the kid wins a fair share. After all, is the history of civilization any more civilized?

COMFY OBJECT AT 12 MONTHS

12

Quiz Biz

You have found, no doubt, that your child is a very hard quiz-master. There is no opportunity to choose a congenial category. You get no sly hints. You don't even get rewarded with a box of the sponsor's product and a thank-you for a grand try when you flub one. The questions run the gamut from the ridiculous ("Daddy, are we rich?") to the sublime ("Daddy, what does God look like?").

You probably manage to rise to the occasion with the ridiculous or the sublime ones, but how about all those questions in between?

Let's take one of these questions—"What is a scallop?" is a pretty average kind of question—and try it on for size. Here are some answers to the question "What is a scallop." Choose one.

    a. "Well . . . they're just scallops, that's all."
    b. "They're seafood."

c. "I don't know."

d. "I don't know, but let's look it up."

If you choose answer *a,* you lose a turn. This is no answer at all, and no self-respecting fiver would let it go at that. If you choose *b,* go back three spaces. You could hardly expect any reasonably bright five-year-old to be satisfied with *b.*

No cigar, either, if your choice is *c.* The parent who offers answer *c* may be on firm moral ground, but is giving up too early in the game. "I don't know" is straightforward and honest once or twice, but if fed a steady diet of answer *c* your kid may decide that you are a couple of dunces, a conclusion most kids don't arrive at until they're at least seven. And if you don't think you are likely to be stumped often enough for it to make any difference, tell us, do *you* know what a scallop looks like before it is plucked from the sea and deep-fat fried into its little brown jacket of bread crumbs?

Which leaves *d.* If *d* is your choice, go to the head of the class. "I don't know, but let's look it up" is your best bet for a number of reasons. Your child will be provided with authoritative answers, will develop confidence in you as an information bureau and won't be so likely to consult with corner cronies when some really delicate question crops up. And besides, you find out some of the damnedest things "looking it up." Did you know, for instance, that the common beaming scallop has a row of tiny eyes around the edge of its shell? These eyes are dark, iridescent blue in color, and glow with a lovely fluorescence. So the next time your relentless quiz-master asks you a toughie, look right back into those lovely fluorescent blue eyes and say: "I don't know, but let's look it up. After we've looked it up, let's all take a nice short nap."

Now, it may be perfectly all right to answer a simple question like why the leaves turn all pretty colors in the fall with a song and dance about Jack Frost skittering about on the North Wind sloshing paint in all directions, but the question of where babies come from and, ultimately, how they got there in the first place deserves an answer of a little more substance. This bit of inquisitiveness is not just the venting of a stray curiosity; the general subject will intrigue your child until Social Security sets in, so you may as well start giving out the word—and some of the words—right now. To the "Why's," resist the temptation to fall back on that last resort, the mechanical and desperate and all-embracing answer, "Because." That's cowardly.

Since stammering, stuttering and rolling your eyes are, at the very least, undignified, it would be well to anticipate some of the more obvious questions so that you can deal with them with at least a modicum of dignity and coherence. The first inquiries into the mysteries of life will come along between the ages of three and four. Just as it is important to avoid a cock-and-bull story which must eventually end in a blind alley, it is important, at least at this point, to avoid any luridly graphic explanations depicting the ripe ovum being pursued up and down mysterious passageways by hordes of darting spermatozoa. Don't let yourself be panicked into exhaustive lectures replete with references to fallopian tubes and complicated further by sweeping tangential references to the birds, the bees and the petunias. After all, all the kid asked was, "Mommy, where do babies come from?"

The answer is very simple: "They grow inside their mommies." Don't bother holding your breath for the next question, because, honest, your child doesn't know you've been backed into a corner.

It's okay if babies grow inside their mommies. The kid just wanted to know. True, there may be a few related questions: "Where do babies grow inside their mommies?" Answer, "Right here." "Is there a baby growing inside of you right now?" Answer, "I don't think so." The kid'll be too busy digesting the material already at hand to proceed to the next point.

These bits of information may rattle about in your tot's uncrowded cranium for weeks before it dawns that there are some loose ends lying around. If your child is the sort that takes things personally, the next question may be, "Did I grow inside of you?" Having no alternative, you answer affirmatively. "How did I get out?" It is becoming clear that Baby is warming up to the subject and is prepared to lay down a barrage worthy of an Inquisitor-General.

"How did I get out, Mommy?"

"Dr. Carter helped you."

"How did I fit inside?"

"Oh, you were very, very little."

"Was I real teeny-weeny?"

"You were real teeny-weeny."

"Like a little froggy?"

"Well, uh, no. As a matter of fact, you were just a seed, and—"

"Like a orange seed?"

"Well, uh—"

"Tangerine seed?"

"Well—"

"Grape seed?"

"W—"

"Watermelon!"

"Please! You'll simply have to stop interrupting if you want me to tell you things. Now, I can understand that you'd like to know how big you were . . . Well . . . Do you remember the geranium seeds you planted in the spring? Well, you were even smaller than that."

"But I growed."

"Yes, you growed. Grew."

"How did I fit after I growed?"

"Grew, dear. Oh, there was room."

"Like my room?"

"Not that kind of room—"

"With wallpaper?"

"Dear, you're interru—"

"And windows?"

"Please!"

"And curtains?"

"Sweety, I just had the grandest idea. How would you like a great big piece of graham-cracker pie?"

And so it will go: Questions and answers and great gobs of graham-cracker pie.

With panel discussions about impotence, the G spot and transvestite rights, and news breaks about rape and mass murder just a channel hop away from Big Bird and Mr. Rogers, it is all but inevitable that you are going to be called upon to answer some other very challenging questions.

You can, to a certain extent, postpone the inevitable by rigorously limiting your child's TV viewing to suitable programming. Channel-hopping can be eliminated by the simple (but expensive) expedient of procuring one of the newer knobless sets and retaining strict control of the "space command" device. But no matter what you do, it follows as surely as the morning after the night before, that as our society binges on even greater openness and freedom of information, parents are going to have to deal with questions that older generations of parents never even asked, much less had to answer.

It is usually possible to frame an appropriate answer on any subject about which a child has managed to frame a question. Keep your answer simple and brief. Sample question and answer: "Mommy, what's test tube babies?" "Well, sweetie, you know how usually babies grow inside the mommy's belly (we *presume* you've already gotten *that* out of the way). Well, some mommies can't get babies started, so scientists and doctors have figured out a way to get the baby started outside the mommy's belly, then put it in afterward."

If the issue in question is a highly controversial one, it may be useful to suggest that different people have different ideas on the subject. If your child wants to know what you think, by all means state your case. Remember, though, that a young child is really not equipped to deal with the emotional head of steam a parent may have built up over the years. Which is to say: Just because you are a nut on a particular subject—dogs running loose, Richard Nixon, zoysia grass—is no reason to saddle your child with your preoccupations.

Sometimes, because of the press of other business or a potentially awkward situation involving other people, it is necessary, even advisable, to postpone the answer to an important question. This is acceptable to most children provided you have a good track record of honoring rain checks. And with really tough questions, a brief postponement offers the advantage of giving you a chance to figure out just what the heck you're going to say.

COMFY OBJECT AT 18 MONTHS

13
Junior Viewers

Ignoring the TV problem is tantamount to consigning your sprout to the intellectual scrap heap. If you are not prepared to deal with it at the outset, you can expect to be superseded in your child's consciousness by the business end of a cathode-ray tube.

While it is true that unlimited viewing by tots results in something like shortening of the medulla oblongata, it does not follow that they should be denied completely the use of the set. The wisest course to follow with your youngster is some sort of rigid supervision. For a child of two or three, a half hour a day is plenty. Some more sedentary small fry can take more, other volatile types not that much. Strict adherence to whatever time limitation seems best for your child is the prime element in your campaign to prevent your pupa from emerging from the cocoon as a witless moth interested in nothing more glowing than the nearest television screen.

Even aside from the important future considerations, this spoon-feeding is of utmost importance. Today's child does not take tele-viewing lightly. Children concentrate on the screen with trancelike intensity. This half hour of transfixion can use up as much energy and imagination as all the rest of a child's day's activities combined. In order to enforce the time limit, it may be expedient to circulate some fiction to the effect that there just isn't any more to be seen. You can switch on an empty channel or two if proof is demanded. In the face of such a convincing demonstration, your child will probably accept your story and be satisfied to acknowledge the incident with a short crying fit and let it go at that. This sort of fabrication may have to be repeated every day for a couple of weeks, but sooner or later your budding viewer will become conditioned to the idea that there is etiquette surrounding Television, just as there is attending Mealtime (sigh of despair), Getting Dressed (groan of anguish) and Bedtime (sob).

During the time your tot's watching TV, attention to such a small detail as the type of chair to be used can contribute to happy viewing. A strong rocking chair is recommended because it affords the child a means of getting rid of the tension that accumulates during the half hour. But even though a child is able to rock off some of the steam, you can expect a volcanic explosion when the fog lifts.

Every child has an individual way of releasing this TV tension. In one case that has come to our attention, the child, a little girl, springs from her hassock and, using the oval braided rug as an indoor track, emulates an Olympic runner. As she tears around the edge of the rug, she whoops like a terrified crane. We advised a rocker in this case, and it seems to have cut down on the whooping. Another child, a boy, would drag his TV rocker into the kitchen, where his parents were sneaking supper, and throw it at his daddy. In this case we prescribed a hassock, and Daddy no longer eats all hunched up. There's no telling what your little cherub may work out. Don't be surprised if the kid simply walks up to you and punches you in the nose.

Once a child shows a real interest in TV it is very easy to fall into the habit of using the set as a sitter. Parents who are conscientious in every other way will often take television on as a kind of built-in sitter without ever considering its qualifications for the job. The quickest way to convince yourself that TV is a bad risk as a sitter is to watch what passes for children's entertainment during a normal week or even for a few days. The difficulty is not that there are no

good children's shows. There are some, though for every really good one there are a dozen mediocre ones and three or four really atrocious ones. The difficulty is simply that a two-year-old is not ready to watch *any* television alone. It is important for the new viewer to have a constant viewing companion, and you are elected. As a youngster's TV guide, it will be up to you to make meaningful what the child can use, and to prevent him or her from being disturbed or confused by what cannot or should not be used. For example: your toddler is watching an excellent network children's show. At the half hour, the host tells the kiddies not to go away, he'll be back in a minute. The nature of TV is such that there's no telling what the local station is going to do with that minute. Your little viewer might see anything from a "public service" spot advocating safe driving, which depicts a ghastly automobile accident, to a commercial for a downtown movie house, which attempts to lure the public away from TV by showing a clip of the current attraction's high spot—two hulking brutes fighting with bullwhips.

Another of your responsibilities as TV guide is to prepare your child for life in the advertising age. With the ad industry directing heavy fire via television, your tot urgently needs to know how and when to duck.

Children who watch too much television and whose viewing is unsupervised often develop a tendency to see the real world in terms of the twelve- or seventeen- or twenty-four-inch screen. The little boy who, upon being told that Uncle Ned died, asked who shot him, wasn't kidding. Neither are the tots who think that people just naturally bash hell out of each other all the time; or that for every reasonably decent law-abiding citizen there are a couple of dozen crooks; that a lion, a tiger, a gorilla, or all three, are just as likely to be lurking around the next corner as not; that, next to squirting stuff under your arms, the most important human activity is drinking beer.

It's true, of course, that small children have always managed to pick up some pretty silly ideas, but until television came along they had to work at it. They had to dig their misapprehensions out of nursery rhymes, fairy tales, magazines, comics and the movies. With

television, all they have to do is sit there. TV is just about the perfect factory for mass-producing crazy mixed-up kids. But you must see to it that, in your case, it doesn't. You've got to train your child to evaluate what's on TV and you must stand by to supply the right frames of reference.

On the other hand, it won't do to turn your tot into a full-fledged agencyphobe—the kid may grow up to be the president of BBD&O, and you wouldn't want to plant the seeds of a deep neurosis. Here are some suggestions for putting a child wise without creating a complete cynic:

1. Explain the whole idea of commercials to your child. Don't be bitter about it. Just explain that they are things put on television by people who want to sell things.

2. Unless a commercial is really objectionable, you should avoid a point-blank attack. The indirect approach is better. Such remarks as, "Do you want to go to the bathroom during this commercial, or do you want to wait until the next one?" and, "Oh, goodie, a commercial! Now we can go get our milk and cookies," will convey the idea.

3. When your child refuses to use the brand of toothpaste you yourself have been using for the last ten years, averring: "You hafta get Mickey Mouse toothpaste! Mickey Mouse toothpaste is the best!" you might say, "Have you ever noticed that on commercials almost everybody says their thing is the best?" Pause. "Well, what that usually means is that they *think* theirs is the best."

The next time somebody tries to tell *your* tot that theirs is the best, you may have the satisfaction of overhearing the response "You jus' *fink* yours is the best!"

4. It is a mistake to give the impression that all TV advertising claims are false or excessive. However, a graphic demonstration that this is sometimes true may provide your child with just the right amount of sales resistance. Suppose, for instance, your youngster has an unreasonable dislike of a certain type of dessert product. Suppose, further, that Uncle Jolly, a favorite TV personality, has announced that this stuff is not only utterly delicious but that it tastes like ice cream, and your child, not recognizing it, has been after you to get some.

This is a perfect setup. Get some with all haste, and serve it, perhaps with some such comment as, "Here's that delicious dessert that tastes just like ice cream that Uncle Jolly is always talking about." Tiny Tot is delighted and piles into it with gusto. But one taste and disillusionment descends. Soon your babe

disconsolately raises spoonsful of the stuff and lets them plop back into the dessert dish. Check the impulse to say, "I told you so." Offer, instead, a nice dish of ice cream.

5. Give credit where credit is due. There are many commercials on television that are worthwhile. If you find a commercial especially interesting or amusing, say so, and encourage your child to do the same.

The animated cartoon has been, almost since the advent of television, the backbone of children's programming. It's not unusual for a three-year-old to watch forty or fifty of the things every week. This is not only too much TV, it is the wrong kind of TV.

Generally speaking, the animated cartoons which are shown on television are very poor material for children under five. In expressing this viewpoint we are no doubt laying ourselves open to a charge of "hogwash." A likely scoff might run: "That stuff never hurt me when I was a kid. Used to see four or five of them every Saturday at the movies." Our answer is that it is one thing to see four or five of them a week at age eight, but quite another to absorb forty or fifty a week at age three. At eight, a child has begun to have a pretty good grip on reality, and is able to recognize the crazy clichés of animated cartoons for the nonsense they are. But the three-year-old is struggling to gain some kind of understanding of the world, and is likely to sponge up any idea he or she can get hold of. A child may want to know what a boat is, for instance. The animated-cartoon definition of a boat is very simple: Boat: a thing that sinks.

We aren't suggesting that a few cartoons will qualify a child for a paragraph in some future edition of Krafft-Ebing or will produce a morbid fear of boats, airplanes, autos, bushes and empty houses. What we are saying is that too many of the wrong kind of cartoons early can seriously handicap a child in the struggle to adjust to the world.

You can prevent your three-year-old from being put off stride by cartoons by educating him or her to see them for what they are. To begin with, as we have said, the fewer seen, the better. You should

view TV with your child, and straighten things out as required. When Krazy Kat's rowboat sinks (Krazy Kat's rowboat *always* sinks), explain in a simple way that in real life boats don't sink. Don't complicate matters by saying that boats don't *often* sink or that they *hardly ever* sink. A three-year-old can absorb either the idea that boats do sink or that they don't. It's much healthier at this stage that the child believe the latter. When Krazy is subsequently pursued by a huge and ferocious shark (Krazy is *always* pursued by a huge and ferocious

shark), remind your child of the real shark you both saw at the aquarium. Because these were a couple of very unimpressive little sand sharks, they can serve as a perfect object lesson.

Bear in mind that it is not your object to spoil the fun. All you need do is establish that Krazy Kat has nothing to do with real life. It would be a healthy thing, too, if your tot were to understand just what animated cartoons are; that is, a great many drawings shown in rapid sequence so as to give an illustion of motion—just as later, when he or she begins watching adventure shows, it will be important to explain the whole concept of actors, sound effects and trick photography.

Demonstrating the principle of the animated cartoon to your three-year-old is as easy as drawing six dots. In fact, that's precisely how it's done—by drawing six dots. Take any magazine. It should be a fairly thick one with some body to it. Open it at random. In the white margin at the top of the right-hand page, about two inches from the right-hand edge, make a black dot. On the next page, a little to the right of where you placed the first dot, place another dot. Repeat this operation until you've got six dots on six succeeding pages, each one a little to the right of the preceding dot. Now, all you have to do is flip the pages. Of course, the dot appears to move. Your child, of course, is delighted; but what is more important, he or she is also enlightened. If you really want to astound your audience, you might refine the demonstration a bit by drawing a wavy line on each of six pages—to represent water. Then go back and draw a little sailboat—a simple triangle will do—on each wave line. Flip the pages, and eureka! the sailboat moves.

Once it's clear that a particular show runs to brutality and violence, declare it out of bounds. Such shows run pretty much to form, and you should be able to evaluate them from a mercifully small sampling. Two or three carefully selected half-hour adventure shows per week are a fair quota for your junior viewer. You ought to watch these shows with your child. When things get tense, mention that you both understand that the bad guy sneaking up on the Solo Ranger is really an actor playing a part. Be careful, though, about making any such comments about the Solo Ranger himself. A brief statement to the effect that of course nothing bad is going to happen to the hero because then there wouldn't be any more shows is about as far as you may go. Remember, you're not there to take the fun out of things but to offer reassurance when the situation gets tense, and to soften the violence in which even the most housebroken of the kiddie adventure shows abound.

Refrain, then, from commenting derisively every time the hero shoots more than six shots from his six-shooter without reloading. That would be carping. You are, however, well within your responsibilities if you explain that the inevitable wild brawls are largely illusory. An extremely graphic demonstration can be produced simply by turning off the sound during one of the fiercer combats. The mighty blows which appear to land so resoundingly are actually misses, and without the powerful suggestion of the sound track, the pretence becomes obvious even to a devoted, bug-eyed little fan. You needn't feel guilty about disabusing your tot of the idea that the good guys and the bad guys are practically killing one another, for, like the lady in the Thurber cartoon, sooner or later we are *all* disenchanted.

The question suggests itself that if TV is such a troublemaker, why let your child watch it at all? Unless you are of the small, embattled group that continues to hold out against television, the question pretty much answers itself. If you've got one of the things in the house—and it's about a hundred to one that you have—you child is going to look at it. And a good thing. For, with all its faults, television has tremendous educational value.

PROGRESS REPORT

Test IV—DRAWING

Examiner offers subject a piece of paper and a crayon and asks child to draw a picture of a man.

CHILD "A"

CHILD "B"

CHILD "C"

CHILD "D"

14

Maintaining Discipline

As your child scrambles through the daily routine, it is inevitable that all that insatiable curiosity will occasionally move down the path of nonproductive behavior. Nonproductive behavior may be defined as acts which have the effect of reducing perfectly good, useful objects to worthless scrap.

Consider how the amount of trash you put out each week has increased as your little wrecking contractor has grown. If these negative tendencies are allowed to flourish unchecked, you may find some day that your entire house has been put out with the trash.

Your whole future may depend on your adherence to a few simple rules *today*. If, already, the neighbors have begun to avoid you on the street, think what it will be like day after tomorrow.

Lay Down the Law
A set of enforceable laws is as necessary to the proper conduct of your home as it is to that of your government. The laws can be very

simple. For instance, "Don't throw the ashtray." As the child probes this ruling for loopholes, it will occur to your little lawyer that you haven't said anything about not *dropping* the ashtray. You must be on the watch for this sort of technical hairsplitting. Before the child can put the thought into action, another law must be shoved into the breach: "Don't *drop* the ashtray." When it's clear that this latest legislation is poorly written and open to considerable interpretive analysis, it proves necessary to draft a third bill which supersedes the two previous ones: "Don't touch the ashtray, or I'll knock your little block off!"

Be Alert for Trouble

There are, of course, certain obvious telltale storm signals which are easily spotted, such as the strident screams of a little girl being snatched baldheaded, the sharp report of a ceramic lamp base

exploding or the enraged roar of an innocent passerby who has been drenched with the hose. In these cases, the parent can arrive quickly at the scene of the crime, sift the evidence and dispense justice.

There are, however, many less obvious portents that can easily escape the notice of the inexperienced parent. Beware the sudden silence in the playroom. Your child is up to something. Spontaneous statements like: "Leo love Mommy. Mommy love Leo?" should be regarded with suspicion. If you notice him quietly reading a book for which he has previously displayed nothing but contempt, listen for the sound of running water. And if you should be advised, "You don't have to buy me a birthday present this year, Mommy," lock him in his room and search the house from top to bottom.

Don't Give In
Never let your child get his own way by means of a temper tantrum. When a tantrum occurs, calmly but firmly remove the child's shoes and put your noisemaker in the crib. Leave the room and close the door. In an hour or two, when the child realizes it is getting no response, the racket will taper off to a hoarse wail. And finally, silence. Waiting out the calm after the storm is universally agreed to be one of the most harrowing experiences of parenthood. Many parents make the mistake of worrying about what the neighbors will think, and after only five or ten minutes of anxious listening, during which they convince themselves that the child has snapped one or more vital blood vessels, they are apt to rush headlong into the room with lollipops and apologies. For these unhappy creatures temper tantrums are daily occurrences and lollipops become a supply problem.

Crime and Punishment
We disagree with Mr. Shaw's dictum that one should never strike a child except in anger. Striking your child, even though the great majority of us do it occasionally, always represents some form of parental failure. As for striking a child in anger, this represents a double failure: failure to control the child and failure to control yourself—a much more serious lapse.

The appropriate punishment for your small miscreant's small misdeeds is prompt, appropriate deprivation of privileges, accompanied by unmistakable expressions of disapproval—even anger if the crime is sufficiently grave.

Truth and/or Consequences

Another of the parent's most important responsibilities is the teaching of the difference between right and wrong. Since none of us always does the right thing, we often find it expedient to cover our deviations from perfection with deviations from truth. Obviously, this is a vicious circle, but it is so firmly superimposed on the family group that we must learn how to live with it.

Here are two simple rules which, although not very golden, can help keep things under control:

1. Don't lie to your child unless it is absolutely necessary.
2. Don't get caught at it.

What constitutes necessity in this matter is something the individual parent must rationalize personally. The child's health and welfare are good criteria. The child's *and* the parents' health and welfare are better ones. There will come Sunday mornings when you will be able to earn yourself an extra hour of sleep simply by convincing your rooster that it *isn't* daytime yet. It may even be expedient to suggest that it's the *moon* that's beaming through the curtains. If you get away with it, it's a lie well spent. Unquestionably it's for the child's own good. With that extra hour of sleep, you'll be able to give a more brilliant reading, later on, of Mickey Mouse, Peanuts and Hagar.

The proper cultivation of some of your child's most important habits will rest squarely on a foundation of lies to the effect that that's what Daddy did when *he* was a little boy: "When Daddy was a little boy, he brushed his teeth three times every day." (Daddy has a complete upper and lower bridge to attest to the fact that his mother often discovered spiderwebs on his toothbrush.) "Daddy always took his vitamins without a fuss. That's why he's so big and strong." (When Daddy was a little boy, vitamins hadn't been invented, and the closest he ever got to his cod liver oil was the time he licked what

he thought was the molasses spoon. As a consequence, Daddy *isn't* very strong, though come to think of it, he *is* getting bigger every day.) "Daddy never left his things lying around when he was finished with them." (Daddy still doesn't put his toys away.)

Even if you are scrupulously careful with your strategic use of the fib as an aid in the rearing of your child, your little Portia will eventually find it is a two-edged weapon and use it against you. You won't have to provide an opportunity to learn the technique by imitation; it occurs to children spontaneously. How you behave in the face of your child's first big fat lie will have a lot to do with the future of wholesale deception in your home.

In many cases the parent forces the child to tell the lie in the first place by insisting on a formal confession of guilt when faced with such irrefutable evidence that a confession is superfluous. If you roar at a three-year-old, "Did you do that?" it won't occur to the tot standing there in front of the marked-up wall holding a red crayon that the question is rather a rhetorical one. He or she will simply weigh the possible answers, and likely decide that "No" is the best bet. If you demand to know who, then, did the foul deed, the child will profess complete bafflement. If you then suggest through gritted teeth that he or she reconsider the plea, your tot is apt, having gotten into the swing of the thing, to come up with a diabolically ingenious whopper.

Resist, therefore, the impulse to undertake the role of prosecuting attorney in cross-examination. When a situation arises that might tempt your child to depart from the truth, don't force the issue. Assume, don't question, the child's guilt. Any normal kid is perfectly capable of thinking up that first lie without any encouragement from you.

Until your child reaches the age of four or so, it will be pretty easy to hear the testimony and deduce the truth. This is likely to create the false but fortunate impression that you are omniscient, reducing considerably your child's inclination to fib. When the time comes for your youngster to rocket out into the world on a tricycle and begin comparing notes with colleagues, however, your feet of clay are in imminent danger of discovery. Not only that, but having whittled you down to size, the child's next step will be to exploit this new knowledge in an intuitive search for your Achilles' heel.

Before you have suffered a complete loss of prestige, however, you can and should embark on a new program calculated to save face all around. This consists of explaining the nice distinction between "lying" and "pretending." It's all right, you say, to "pretend" up to a point—so long as you both know that's all it is; but if the child tries to make the story stick, the game falls flat and you won't have any. If you play your cards right, you'll find that things will go more or less smoothly. Your youngster tells you a palpable untruth; there follows a stimulating battle of wits as stylized as a Chinese drama; then you say, "Okay, now tell me what *really* happened at Debbie's house this afternoon." Chances are you'll get the straight dope. And that's all there is to it—except to phone Debbie's mother and assure her that she is welcome to use your Mixmaster while hers is being repaired.

15

First Outings

Eventually your child will become sufficiently aware that there is a big wonderful world out there, so there is nothing for it but to screw up your courage and undertake some outings.

Perhaps the most important thing to remember in dealing with children is that no two of them are alike. Advice and handy-dandy rules (like these) are useful only if you adapt them to the needs of your particular child. There *are* children who are so sturdily (or insensitively) constituted that they need very little preparation for anything—and there are those at the other extreme who need a scenario at every turn of the road. But most kids fall into that middle range that includes most of us—individuals who would like to have

149

some idea just what the heck is going to happen next. A little sensible preventative orientation can not only save you and your child a certain amount of upset, but may even head off a few galloping traumas at the pass.

This raises the issue of doing whatever it is you have to do to make your little charge presentable.

If your special problem is a little boy, you are probably wondering what to do about his hair, and—with justice—dreading the ordeal. Except for the rare little numbskull who will stand for anything, the first haircut will be sorely needed long before he will accept the ministrations of a professional barber.

Cutting Baby's hair is just a shade easier than bathing a tomcat. You will need help, all the help you can get. Can the man next door dance a jig? Have him in. Can the mailman make a noise remarkably like a cannon by clicking his tongue against the roof of his mouth? Urge Officer Callahan to come sample your latest culinary triumph. Of course, if Daddy is the only entertainment you can get, you'll have to make do.

The workman being no better than his tools, you should obtain the best pair of scissors you can find. If these happen to be snaggle-toothed affairs which have to be screwed together every three snips, well, chin up: there's no turning back now.

Some other things it might be good to have on hand are: an unlimited supply of ice cubes, a large box of lollipops, piles of old newspaper, a bunch of old ladies' hats (preferably the kind with a lot of net and ostrich feathers), some large paper bags, two ripe bananas, a box of corn flakes and a big pile of assorted kitchen utensils, old jewelry, sewing scraps and bits of string.

The idea is for Daddy to fascinate him while Mommy cuts his hair. The cutting job requires a surgeon's steady hand, the nerves of a steeplejack and inhuman patience. The haircutter must anticipate the subject's every move. Beginning at the back, working around each side, then pruning the front, each snip should be made with an eye to the total effect.

Daddy's job, on the other hand, requires only tremendous endurance and a boundless imagination. Any gymnastic or juggling ability he may have is definitely to the good. An important aspect of Daddy's end of the job is pacing; like a prizefighter, he must conserve his strength so he can go the distance. He should begin with easy things like putting on funny hats, and save the hard stuff, like tripping and falling heavily against the china closet, till last.

Daddy must be acutely sensitive to the demands of his audience. Interest must not be allowed to wane even momentarily. Suppose, for instance, Daddy has hit on the happy device of tearing newspapers into long shreds and letting them float gently to the floor. If, after a bit of this, a certain restiveness is observed, Daddy must vary his routine. Instead of dropping the streamers to the floor, he might begin to eat them, producing with each swallow an intriguing noise like that made by plucking a loose guitar string. The little fellow will soon be chuckling happily again as his mother chops away with desperate concentration.

As you can see, the haircutting problem is one of formidable proportions. There are no simple directions on the package. It is a difficult task, but not a thankless one. For, as you crouch wearily amidst the debris, a wonderful sight may be described through the settling haze of hair. It's your son—and he looks like a *real boy*!

If you're the parent of a girl, of course, you probably don't have to cope with the haircut problem. But before you start gloating, consider this: all the haircuts from now through puberty won't add up to the cost of one wedding.

In any case, now that the child is presentable, it's time to go somewhere.

TRIP TO THE ZOO

On any given sunny Sunday it occurs simultaneously to thousands of parents that the time is ripe for that first trip to the zoo. Blinded by their own brilliance, these ill-fated people fail to see the projected jaunt as anything but unalloyed delight. In their exhilaration they do not realize that the beauties of the zoological garden flourish in quicksand.

For our purposes, the zoo may be likened to a golf course. Each is scientifically laid out so as to test to the full a person's skill and endurance. With each there is a series of tests: in golf there are eighteen holes; in zoo-going there are the dozens of exhibits. Also similarly, the field of activity in each is generously laced with traps and hazards—sand and water on the one hand and refreshment stands selling peanuts, popcorn, Cracker-Jack, hot dogs, soda pop, souvenirs and gas-filled balloons on the other. For the tyro the two enterprises even share the same aftereffects: general exhaustion, blistered feet, extremely sore legs from having walked great distances and a sense of frustration—the result of having fallen far short of a lofty goal.

You won't learn here how to break a hundred, but the following material may help you in your determination to see that the first trip to the zoo results in an accord between your child and the beasts of the jungle, the wood and the plain.

The Elephant House
Parents are often bewildered when their little one emits a piercing howl at the first sight of an elephant. "That's strange," Mommy says

to Daddy. "The little woolly blue elephant that cousin Ethel gave him has always been one of his favorite toys." The only strange thing about it is that Mommy and Daddy should be so obtuse as to expect Baby to see any similarity between the little woolly blue toy and this great gray monster. It's of no use to tell him not to be afraid; that's not why he's crying. He's bawling because he feels horribly, utterly betrayed. Since it was received about a year ago, the little blue puff has been universally referred to as an elephant. Now, after having been told over and over that he was going to see a real live elephant at the zoo, here he is confronted with this ugly, outsized imposter. It's enough to put anybody off stride.

The Lion House

Oliver Goldsmith, poet, playwright, essayist and naturalist, in his work *Animated Nature,* 1825 edition, has this to say about lions: ". . . though he usually feeds on fresh provision, his urine is insupportable." Don't be embarrassed if, as you enter the crowded lion house, your two-year-old loudly paraphrases and corroborates Mr. Goldsmith. It is merely the first of many candid observations your child will make during the afternoon, so you might as well be calm about it. If your child is one of the many whose first sight of the King of Beasts is greeted with less than bubbling enthusiasm, let it go at that and be on your way. Do not under any circumstances sweep the tot from the stroller in order to supply a better look at the terror of the veldt. Don't bother to explain that the lion is a sweet old thing

who simply *loves* little children; this will just confirm all the worst fears. Saunter down to the other end of the building to see some of the smaller members of the cat family. A black panther sleeping at the rear of a cage is a good beginning; or if you want to play it absolutely safe, locate the tabby that is kept about the place to keep down the mice.

The Reptile House

Your zoo will doubtless boast a prize collection of slithery snakes, crawly lizards and warty crocodiles. It is important, as you conduct your child through the reptile house, to avoid making any remarks which might betray your own unhealthy fear of slithery snakes, crawly lizards and warty crocodiles. You don't want your child saddled with such a shamefully medieval attitude, so be sure to smile sweetly at every revolting thing you see, remarking brightly through gritted teeth on how *pretty* the markings are. After you're outside, you can get off by yourself and have a good "Ugh!"

The Monkey House

Having conceded at the outset that Daddy looks like the Barbary ape and Mommy like the sooty mangabey, there is fun for the entire family here. You can have a fine time spotting in-laws while your offspring attempts to analyze the strange appeal of the Barbary ape and the sooty mangabey; but be prepared to pull up stakes and go at the first indication that the dear little simians intend to help the tot's analysis along with a practical demonstration. This uninhibited expression of a vernal impulse will assuredly give rise to observations from your youngster surpassing in candor anything he or she has said so far all day or is likely to say for months to come. If this happens, you have only two courses of action open to you, neither of them enviable: either pretending not to hear and keeping mum or else launching then and there into an indoctrination lecture that will be a source of interest not only to your offspring but to an entire audience of several dozen highly amused onlookers.

The Small-Mammal House
With its teeming population of raccoons, beavers, skunks, possums and woodchucks, the small-mammal house is an ideal place for your young zoologist. These very animals are the heroes of virtually all children's books and records, so no child will have much difficulty recognizing them; but even in this paradise things can go amiss. On one occasion a mink-coated young mother pointed to the little mink at which her three-year-old daughter was marveling and informed her, "It took 278 of those little things to make this coat." The kid cried off and on for eighteen years until her old man bought her a mink coat of her own.

But it is growing late, and so, our little naturalist stuffed full of peanuts, popcorn, Cracker-Jack, hot dogs and soda pop, our expedition heads home, while a gas-filled balloon, having come loose from its mooring on a small thumb, continues its loudly lamented ascent slowly toward the golden heavens.

TRIP TO THE RESTAURANT

You have taken your small child "out to eat." The hostess seems to recognize you as she inquires, "How many?" Making a quick count, you answer in a voice that seems hardly your own, "Three." As you are conducted to a far corner table, it all comes back to you—the hostess, the quick count. . . . The same compulsion which causes the criminal to return to the scene of the

*crime has drawn you to the very restaurant which was the site
of your previous experiment in eating out with Baby. Recollec-
tions flood in on you hideously—the shattered high chair, the
hurtling saltcellar, the sea of spilt milk. . . . Somehow you are
seated. The hostess scurries away as a waitress approaches.
Before you can say her nay she adds to the already abundantly
set table three brimming glasses of ice water. A shout sticks in
your throat like a giant oyster cracker as Baby grabs a corner
of the tablecloth and whisks it off the table. There is an ava-
lanche of silverware, a tidal wave of ice water, and sugar cubes
are flung across the mystic bowl of night.*

—Dream, common in parents of small children.

The best advice on the subject of taking small children "out to eat"
is not to; but if you are one of the vast majority unable to get it
through your head that eating out is just another of life's little pleasures that was automatically crossed off the list when you took on
parenthood, you may be interested in some suggestions for making
the best of a bad situation.

1. Never take a hungry child to a restaurant. Blunt the appetite with milk and cookies before you leave the house. This will serve a double purpose: the child is far less likely to be irritable and, having already got milk into your tot, you can afford to be generous about ginger ale while you're waiting for the food to come. Then, of course, there is the added advantage that your wee one will have the opportunity for leg-stretching during your consequential trips to the rest room.

2. Choose a nearby restaurant. A long drive improves no one's humor, least of all a hungry child's. So don't try out that wonderful place forty miles up the pike that Bill and Cora have been raving about. Save it for some night when you've invested in a sitter.

3. Order something for your youngster that is ready to serve. A meatball in the hand is worth two lamb chops queued up in the kitchen.

4. Never stand in line for a meal. Since your child's reaction to the whole business of eating is at best one of bored toleration, the notion of standing in line to be permitted to sit down to a meal is likely to seem so utterly outrageous that he or she may run amok.

5. Keep it gay. If you are relaxed and pleasant, chances are your youngster will at least make a stab at following your example. By the same token, if your gay smile begins to wear thin as things drag on, your child will sense your impatience and sour on the whole operation. And don't count on the Muzak to drown out the protests.

One last bit of advice: If the waitress is empowered to ask if you'll have something to drink, by all means have something. A Scotch on the rocks will raise your feeling-no-pain threshold just enough so that the spilled tomato juice won't feel quite so icky as it drizzles down your leg. Even if you have to drive and it has been truly said of you that "one" puts you on your ear, order it anyway, for the next hour or so is going to be, at best, a sobering experience.

TRIP TO THE MOVIES

Your local Cinema 4 (four theaters, lots of waiting—especially for the rare film that's reasonably appropriate for kids) is a confusing, chaotic place with a vast parking lot usually accessed from a major highway notorious for drag races and jackknifed tractor trailers. So far not so good—not for you and certainly not for your three-to-four-year-old.

Now, consider the theater experience itself. You go into a long, dimly lit room with a mixed bag of imperfect strangers, some bent on fun, some bent on mischief, some just bent. *Then the lights go out and it's pitch dark*. It's enough to scare the living cement out of any self-respecting youngster. Remember, this is the kid who won't even consider going to sleep without a night-light.

Perish forbid you should be so foolhardy as to arrive *after* the lights are out. Finding a seat in a crowded darkened theater is a traumatic experience when you are on your own, but with a small terrified child on your hip—your child will quite sensibly insist on being carried after one look at the situation—it's the sort of shin-kicking, instep-crunching experience that nightmares are made of and could, at the very least, get you lynched.

Now consider the choice of film. There is not a single classic children's film that does not include material that is virtually certain to scare hell out of your three-to-four-year-old—not *Snow White*, not *Pinnochio*, not *Bambi*, not *Dumbo*, not *ET*, not etc. Oh, come on, you say. Those are great films, and to deprive children of them would be almost criminal! Who's depriving?

Are we proposing that you desist taking your tot to these great films? Not at all. We know perfectly well that you can't wait to see them again yourself. (We couldn't—we've seen *Snow White* eleven times. Our favorite part is during the dwarfs' dance when Sneezy blows Dopey to the rafters with a giant ah-choo.)

We are suggesting delay, not deprivation. Why not wait until your child is six, seven or eight to deal with the really terrifying witch in *Snow White*, the Pleasure Island sequence in *Pinnochio* (shades of Kafka!), the death of Bambi's father, the bad guys after ET or the tragic separation of Dumbo from his mother? What we propose, simply and humbly, are some preventative measures, along with

some suggestions about how to cope if and when things threaten to get out of hand.

1. Prepare your child for the experience. The fact that a movie house is dark is taken for granted by adults. But it could come as a disconcerting shock to an unsuspecting tot.

2. While there's no need to impose a total silence rule, point out that while the movie experience bears some similarity to the TV experience, there are differences, and that out of respect for the other patrons your child should keep a zippered lip at least some of the time . . .

3. —except when it's open to receive popcorn, M&Ms (at *ET,* of course, Reese's Pieces are *de rigueur*) or such other comestibles that you have chosen to keep your child quiet. Jujubes are especially good as they tend to gum up the mouth and inhibit speech.

4. Do not sit close to the screen. The witch in *Snow White* is scary enough from way back; up close, she's instant nightmares.

5. If your child wants to watch the movie with ears covered and face buried in your bosom during the scary parts, by all

means allow it. It's a nice close feeling. Under no circumstances should you mock, tease or call your child scaredy-cat. If you do, there's got to be a special place for you in the Inferno.

6. If at some point your child asserts that it's time to go home, give the proposition serious consideration. It may prove the better part of valor.

TRIP TO THE MALL

Shopping malls are second only to airports in the inordinacy of the amount of walking they require for the accomplishment of what would seem to be a simple purpose—entering an aircraft in the one case, buying provender in the other. A collapsible stroller, therefore, is very much in order, at least until your youngster absolutely insists on negotiating solo. Shopping with an infant or very small child is not much better or worse an experience than doing anything in public with an infant or very small child. It usually consists of accepting the applause of the crowds for having produced such a darling chin-chuckable little child while hoping you can get the whole miserable thing over with before the little darling gets sopping enough to just float away.

When your child reaches tothood and develops an independent mind and will, different sorts of problems present themselves. Here are some of the most frequent ones along with some ideas on how they might be dealt with.

Galloping Gimmies at the Toy Store
Malls are rife with marvelous toy stores featuring fabulous displays of precisely the toys your little gimme artist has been nagging you for since Santa forgot to bring them last Christmas. It is important and necessary that you establish, as early as possible, a workable set of rules for dealing with toy-lust in the marketplace. Fortunately, most children are capable of understanding the general idea of limits—the idea that for a variety of reasons none of us—not your child, not you, not even Daddy—can have everything we want when we want it. There are limits relating to money ("Mommy just doesn't have enough money, sweetheart, to buy you that forty-nine dollar 'Wide

World of Monsters' playset."), limits based on age-appropriateness (". . . and besides, you're much too young, sweetie, for 'Wide World of Monsters'—the parts are so little they might get stuck in your little throat."), limits arising out of considerations of taste (". . . not to mention the fact that I wouldn't consider having the disgusting things in my house!"), and finally, limits based on the exhaustion of patience

("... and if you don't stop that damn whimpering, I'm going to knock your little block clear into the parking lot!").

A reasonable and workable compromise could involve letting your tot buy some inexpensive toy or book during these grueling treks to the mall. The prospect of such a goodie will do wonders for your child's humor and tractability.

The Getting Lost Syndrome

Children vary considerably in their ability to get lost. Some kids can get lost on their way to the bathroom in their own house, while others can maintain a sense of direction and location in a vasty mall. Here are some thoughts on dealing with the great middle ground of youngsters who are capable of getting lost but don't necessarily make a habit of it, along with some ideas and techniques that may save you a few trips to the mall's lost-child station:

1. Some article of very brightly colored clothing—day-glo isn't very chic, but it sure is visible—will not only help keep your tot within eyeshot in a crowded mall, but also has a certain panache.

2. Most children have a tendency to be trailers. The reason for this is that walking behind Mommy allows the child to keep her in view. The trouble with this is that small children are very easily distracted and, since most mommies' legs look pretty much alike, the child is likely to resume following the wrong pair after even a brief distraction.

In an uncrowded situation, you might give your child the responsibility of "leading the way"—then *you* keep your *child* in view.

In crowded mall situations, it is necessary either to hang on to your child or have your child hang on to you. Or, if that is impossible because your arms are filled with the day's plunder, just sort of dribble the kid ahead of you like a soccer ball.

3. Most children who wander off in shopping situations do so out of sheer boredom while Mommy is selecting or trying on merchandise. A simple ploy here is to promote involvement in the experience, perhaps by appointing your youngster guardian of some small purchase. Children are fiercely possessive— yours may put Cerberus to shame guarding your panty hose purchase.

The Pet Store Hazard

The most hazardous hazard at the mall is the pet store—guaranteed to be jam-packed with adorable little animals just waiting to fall in love with your child at first sight. Avoid it as the plague. If you do not, your home will become a landlocked ark filled with animals (and animal problems) of every kind. Of course, if you already have a large dog, a couple of cats, some gerbils, some fish and a parakeet, by all means drop by the pet store. It might be diverting to see some animals you don't have to clean up after for a change.

SUPERMARKET SAFARI

As a general rule, kiddies under three should be cart-ridden. The one-year-old who is permitted to explore the supermarket on foot will quickly find the way to the low bins of the vegetable counter to see eye to eye with the potatoes. Unless yours is in serious need of minerals, too many unwashed spuds may have an undesirable effect on a child's metabolic balance. Similarly, the unchauffered two-year-old will lose no time in discovering the cookie counter. As a result, you will kill the better part of your shopping session by having to restack its entire contents.

When your child is old enough, he or she should be allowed to help. Definite assignments—one at a time—are in order. Unless briefed in this fashion, the acquisitive four-year-old may be responsible for fifteen or twenty unspecified items turning up among your groceries at the checker's stall. At this point, you either pay your money and take your goods, or you ignore the line piling up behind you and take time out to eliminate such choice surprises as a half-dozen giant rat traps, a quart of pine jelly soap, one hundred yards of plastic clothesline and a half-gallon jar of brandied persimmons.

To sum up: the very best rule to follow with regard to visiting the marts of trade with your youngster in tow is—Don't.

COMFY OBJECT AT 24 MONTHS

16
Creativity

A child reaching the age of two begins to feel the urge to create. Catching this creative instinct at the time of its first stirrings and channeling it intelligently will contribute greatly toward keeping your family ship on an even keel. You may assume that the time for channeling has arrived when your youngster encompasses some grand inventive scheme by wreaking havoc on a useful, even treasured, household object. Entering the living room to see what that odd noise is, you discover your wee one standing on the stair landing, violently belaboring the newel post with a prized needlepoint sofa cushion. It has come open at one corner, and tiny white feathers fill the air. Beaming, your tot announces, "Look, Mommy, I making *snow*!"

An ideal creative toy for the two-year-old is a good supply of modeling clay. The clay available at most toy stores is put up in sets of colored strips. Before you present it to your two-year-old, however, you must mash all those lovely bright strips together until you have a uniform gray glob. The purpose of this preliminary kneading is to save your little sculptor the frustrating experience of having all the pretty colors neutralize right before those stricken eyes. Otherwise, as little Rodin begins to roll out a snake and the colors merge into a dull gray, "It pupposed to be a *green* nake!" the whimper will

come, the eyes welling with tears. So it's much simpler to begin with a big unesthetic lump. Such a lump contains the makings of approximately thirty-two snakes of varying sizes and family relationships. When the tiny artist has manufactured a big granddaddy snake all of ten feet long and dragged the giant reptile clear into the kitchen via the living room and dining room to allow you the privilege of first gander, it's time to allow some branching out into other media for a while.

When your young Picasso is able to identify a particular scribble with a particular image in the mind's eye, he or she has a perfect right to announce the creation of a picture. It may be just a slight variation of the scribble your child has been producing for months, but if now you are proudly informed that it represents a kangaroo skipping rope in a snowstorm, take the kid's word for it.

When your minor master deigns to show one of these masterpieces, regard it attentively. If the title of the work is not volunteered, it's perfectly good form to ask what the picture is supposed to be. Perhaps upon being told it's a picture of a "whole bunch of giraffes eating the tops off the trees," you are able to detect some element of the picture which seems to bear this out. At which point you might play a long shot and say, "Oh, yes, I see their big long necks." If it pays off, fine. But if the artist straightens up to his or her full

twenty-seven inches and says in a hurt, indignant tone: "No! That's their *teefs*! Their necks is over *here*!" beat a fast apologetic retreat and keep the incident in mind when next you are tempted to leap to a naive conclusion.

Resist, as well, the temptation to offer the artist constructive criticism. Your particular artist simply cannot use it. Another pitfall to avoid in your role of patron of the arts is flattery. If you are indiscriminately and excessively enthusiastic, you may find yourself written off as a well-meaning but soft-headed old party whose comments are hardly worth soliciting.

It is important that the tools which you place at your child's disposal keep pace with need. The mother who tries to play safe by restricting her child to pencil and bridge pad when the creative urge requires more soul-stirring things is just asking for trouble. Little Michelangelo may emerge from the bedroom at some small hour and turn an expensive papered room into a private Sistine Chapel. Not having paints, the budding artist will have to make do with what's around the house, and may discover that mustard, catchup and plum jam are excellent paint substitutes. They come in handsome decorator colors and have sufficient covering power to require only one coat. No brush or roller needed; you just smear it on with your hands.

After your child works through pencils, crayons and chalk and slate, it may be time to bestow the accolade of paints and brushes. The paints could be some reasonably yielding set of "hard" colors in a paintbox. (Test the color with a moistened finger. If no color comes off, ask to see something else.) Another excellent solution, if you are willing to risk opaque liquid water color in jars (variously called tempera, gouache or show-card color), is to buy some basic colors and pour out just enough for one session. An ordinary muffin tin makes an excellent receptacle.

A good place to shop for brushes is the paint counter of the five-and-ten. It is usually stocked with a variety of low-priced round ferrule brushes. These are inexpensive and will bear up almost as well under your small fry's swab-the-deck technique as quality brushes costing many times more.

Here are a couple of tricks that will help keep your painter in paper at no expense and with little trouble. Select the three or four pages from each issue of the daily newspaper that carry no large ads or pictures—the want-ad, classified and editorial pages, for instance. Stash these away daily and you'll be ready when your youngster goes on a painting spree. At the beginning of a painting career a child is not likely to resent the fact that the paper is less than pristine. Then, too, newspaper is wonderfully absorbent, facilitating a swoop-down and sop-up operation if the muse of painting is in imminent danger of death by drowning.

If you are a bag saver (and who isn't?), you are in an excellent position when the young master's willingness to paint on old news-papers shreds to resentment. Simply smooth out a large brown paper bag, and cut the bottom off. Slit it down one side and open it out flat. You will have provided a surprisingly large piece of heavy-duty drawing paper. If you are a big saver worthy of the name you should be set for some time to come.

PROGRESS REPORT

Test V—EXAMINING A BOOK

The examiner offers the subject the book and suggests that the subject look at it.

CHILD "A"

CHILD "B"

CHILD "C"

CHILD "D"

17
Day Care

Some things about the experience of parenthood haven't changed very much—the miracle of tiny fingers and toes hasn't changed at all, the fretful bane of colic and the angst of teething have been preserved intact.

But some things do change—rapidly and radically. In the past twenty years, the number of working mothers in the population has grown from 17 percent to 50 percent. This enormous change raises many issues, not the least of which is the matter of child care. What, years ago, was generally a judgment call—will nursery school be good for little Jill or Johnny, is he or she too young, is there a shortage of kids in the neighborhood, etc.—has become for many parents as urgent a necessity as food and shelter.

Indeed, finding adequate child care so you can keep on working has a considerable bearing on whether you will be able to *afford* food and shelter in this perpetually inflationary society.

If you are part of the minority that still has the option of choosing whether to use day care or not, you should start by considering your own particular situation.

Nursery schools do serve a vitally important function. They afford the child, who might not otherwise have it, an opportunity to play and work in the company of a reasonably representative cross section of kids. *How* representative is, of course, a question for the parent to look into when selecting a school. It's not just a matter of the child's day-to-day fun. A four-year-old *needs* the company of children of similar age.

If your neighborhood has an abundance of prekindergarteners and enough play space to accommodate their burgeoning activities, there's no need to send your youngster to nursery school. The parent

who sends a child to nursery school simply as a matter of course is not giving the kid a fair shake. If circumstances are such that a child can develop happily and healthily at home, then, generally speaking, the child is better off there.

Too many three- and even two-year-olds are sent to nursery school simply because a baby has arrived on the scene. The parents of these tots may pay abundant lip service to the idea that it is important for children to have brothers and sisters, but in practice they follow a policy of rigid segregation. "How is Jackie getting along with his new baby sister?" Jackie's mother is asked.

"Oh, just beautifully!" she gushes, adding: "Jackie's in nursery school from nine till three-thirty. Then he watches TV from three-thirty 'til supper, then after supper the baby goes to bed. Oh, yes, it's working out beautifully. There's just one trouble. He keeps trying to get at her in the morning before he goes to school. But even that's no real problem. His daddy's still home at that time, so there are two of us to watch him."

That the four-year-old is not entirely ready for school is argued by the fact that the weight of professional experience indicates that five is the age at which kindergarten becomes feasible. At five, children start liking the feeling of being part of a group. They enjoy learning songs together. Buttons and bows come within their ken. And nineteen out of twenty five-year-olds are good bets to make it to the bathroom every time.

All the disadvantages, both inherent and extrinsic, to the contrary notwithstanding, if your child doesn't have playmates of the same age and if your neighborhood is uncongenial, nursery school can contribute much toward development. Just as there are situations in

which nursery school is obviously not needed, under other combinations of circumstances nursery school may be the *only* answer.

Which brings us back to the majority of parents in this country. Here are some of the factors to be considered when choosing a day-care facility. As with so many of the problems and concerns of parenthood, common sense is much more important than special knowledge.

Visit the Facility While It's in Session

One big reason for starting your nursery-school shopping early is to be able to visit the school while it's in session. Call or write the schools you are considering, explaining that you may wish to enroll your child next September and that you'd like to pay a visit. Headmasters usually prefer to take the parent of prospective enrollees on a nice quiet after-hours guided tour of the "plant" with much attention paid to equipment, feeding facilities and the like. Make it clear that you want to see the school in action.

If management would prefer a cozy chat in the administrator's office after the evidence has all gone home, regard the establishment with suspicion.

Observe the nature of the interaction between the kids and the care-giving staff. Do the kids generally appear to like the "teachers"? Is there plenty of unforced cuddling and comforting of the kids who seem to want it and need it, and a respectful "hands off" policy for kids who prefer to interact in other ways—like beating the teacher at chess, for example?

Don't expect to find a nursery school where seldom is heard a discouraging word and calmness and quietude reign. There is no

such. Four-year-olds have a natural flair for anarchy, and there are bound to be altercations. What you want to find out is how they are handled. What does the teacher do when Eugene walks up to Sally and smashes her over the head with a bucket of sand? Does she make it damn clear that we just don't do things like that in this school, or does she put her arm around the little monster and say sweetly: "Now, Eugene, Sally doesn't want to play that game now. I'll tell you what! Suppose you come in and help me put out the soup for lunch." If sweet talk seems to be the order of the day rather than just desserts, you'd better ask yourself how your youngster is going to fit into the picture. Will he understand that Eugene behaves atrociously because he "suffers from feelings of insecurity," and that the school is "helping him with his problem by giving him the feeling that he is loved?" He will not! What he will understand is that the way to get to help with the soup is to smash Sally over the head with a bucket of sand. Beware of the sort of school that prides itself on being able to do wonders with "difficult children." All too frequently the wonders are performed to the detriment of the kids whose parents have led—or dragged—them more or less in the ways of righteousness.

Don't Believe Everything You Read

It has been said that every business is a people business. In no area is this more to the point than in the matter of choosing a day-care facility. The quality and quantity of personnel is much more important than the latest word in plant and equipment. It's people who care for children—not stainless steel mini-kitchens and mint collections of Fisher-Price preschool toys. It takes a tremendous amount of teacher power to operate a nursery class of four-year-olds. For example, for the conscientious nursery-school teacher the rigors of winter are stupefying. From the first frost to the first robin the kids come to school accoutred in a collection of boots, galoshes, snowpants, leggings, storm coats, parkas and ponchos fit for, at the very least, an expedition to one of the poles. It is practically impossible for one teacher to get twenty or so four-year-olds out of and back into the correct clothes. It's a brute of a job for two or three teachers.

Much more difficult to assess than the quantity of supervision at a nursery school is the quality. You can find out about teacher *quantity* simply by asking, but it's not that easy to determine teacher *quality*. It's true that the school catalog provides a background on each member of the faculty—schooling, experience and so on—but unless you have an almost professional knowledge of the field such credentials won't tell you much. For example, the dossier on Miss Hilary Flute might read: "Miss Flute, who has taught our nursery class of four-year-olds for the past two years, comes to us from four years of teaching at the Beaver Valley Suburban Day School in Chillicothe, Ohio. She earned her degrees at Pestalozzi State Teachers' College." Chances are this history indicates eight to ten years of the soundest kind of training and experience, but, on the other hand, what's to prevent Pestalozzi State from having been a hotbed of wildly progressive educational theory and Beaver Valley Suburban Day from having been the kind of place where the teachers stand around discussing abnormal child psychology while the kiddies pistol whip each other with the six-shooters they brought in for "Show and Tell"? If the catalog poop sheet is only the sketchiest kind of guide (it *does* tell you if the ink is dry on the teachers' certificates), how *can* you tell about the teachers at a given school? You'll just have to patch together a working opinion from what you see at the school. You should, for instance, get a distinct impression that the teachers are in control of the children.

Seek First-Hand-Experience Recommendations
from Parents You Know and Trust
When seeking good child care—or a good gynecologist, acupuncturist or divorce lawyer, for that matter—there is no substitute for the recommendations of fellow-sufferers who have been there. You can talk to people who have sent theirs to the particular school. It's one of those rare legitimate occasions for taking it upon yourself to bother perfect strangers. After this systematic program of spying, prying, probing and snooping, you should be able to come up with a reasonably well-informed guess as to which school your child should attend come next semester. An added advantage to planning things far in advance is that you'll have the whole summer to figure out how you're going to scrape up the tuition.

Does the Space and Operational Format of the Facility
Allow for a Flexible, Interactive Schedule?
Day care works best when children are permitted to move in and out of various types of activities as their individual needs and attention spans require—perhaps quiet puzzle play for a while, then maybe a quick dip into the maelstrom of action play, then perhaps a little role-playing in Doll Corner.

Of course, there is a need for an overall schedule involving such events as opening class, mealtime, nap time, snack time, story hour, etc., but it is the substructure created by the individual child that gives that sense of autonomy that even the youngest toddler needs.

The Mayhem Factor
During your visit to a prospective day care center, make a rough count of cuts, bruises, black eyes and broken limbs in the school

population. If the count is impressive, ask questions. If answers are not forthcoming, or run to glib commentaries on the issue of over-protectiveness, be forewarned.

Not that a school population that looks like the Wild Bunch is *necessarily* disqualifying. If your youngster is of a type more likely to give than to receive, you may figure *c'est la guerre* and sign up.

Now that it's all settled, you can get down to the business of worrying about how your toddler is going to take to the whole idea. You can even lie awake a few nights as the first day of school approaches if you tend to do that sort of thing. But *don't,* by word, deed or facial expression, communicate your concern to your child. A four-year-old who is "ready" for school will take to it like the proverbial duck. The school will probably tell you how they want the first day "handled." With four-year-olds attending school for the first time, most schools like to have the parent come and stay until the child makes it clear that it's all right to go home. This knowledge is communicated in various ways. Your child may surprise you by sending you packing almost immediately with a big kiss good-bye and a "See you later!" But don't be disturbed if the child wants you to hang around for a while and seems to prefer a sub rosa departure with him or her looking the other way while you sneak out.

Occasionally a child who really is ready for nursery school will make more of a production of letting Mommy or Daddy go home than seems appropriate. We don't mean the pitiful ones who are palmed off onto the school by derelict parents. These children have a legitimate beef against school or any other medium of their parents' delinquency, and are going to show their resentment one way or another. We refer to the child, who for reasons probably not even the child knows, wants you to come to school the *second* day, too. Don't get panicky if your child is one of these. Play along for a while. When it turns out that you're the only parent still hanging around, your youngster is apt to realize how silly you look standing there and give you your walking papers. Probably your tot will ride a school bus, and it's a big help toward getting things off to a good start if you see to it that he or she rides the bus to school the first day. A nice ride on the school bus is the pleasantest kind of initiation into the group, and the sooner your child identifies with the class, the easier will be the transition to school life. However, you should be at the school to meet the bus.

If your child goes off to nursery school with a good guard up and comes home rent and spent, it shouldn't take you long to figure out that he is not "making out" at school. On the other hand, if he or

she zooms off each morning with the zest of a soldier of fortune taking off for a Central American revolution and returns with the air of conquering hero, it's a simple deduction that he or she is "making out" just fine. Chances are, however, that your child represents neither of these extremes but, instead, goes to school more or less willingly and returns more or less in one piece.

While you may be able to garner a few bare facts by point-blank questioning—"We play with blocks"; "One of the toilets is stopped up"; "The bus driver has a red hat"—you will probably find out little or nothing about how your adventurer is "making out." In fact, he or she may seem puzzled and resentful at all the questioning, and clam up completely. It's not surprising that a child should react this way. In the first place, for four years your tot has been building an image of you as a remarkable person—omnipotent, omnipresent and omniscient—and here you are twitching like an idiot, slavering over such irrelevancies as the color of the bus driver's hat. Another reason for resentment may be that your child very likely doesn't know *how* to tell you what happened at school today. The relating of one's experiences is a skill in which the average four-year-old has had little or no practice. The technique of getting a small child to "open up" involves three elements. The first, aimed at perpetuating the myth of your omniscience, calls for the use of simple guesswork. The next two, the Leading Question and the Loaded Question, are designed to overcome the witness's limited ability to tell you what you want to know. Do not, in the first instance, try to convince a child that you have full and complete knowledge of all school experiences; just try to give the idea that you have a pretty good idea of what goes on and that you need all this information merely to fill in the details and the proper names. You might begin by guessing the names of classmates. Simply by sticking to some such common names as John, James, William, Mary, Anne and so on, you're bound to come up with a few bull's-eyes—as many as five or six, with any luck at all. Since that's probably more than your child can remember, he or she will be impressed and pleased with your performance, and won't see any significance in the fact that you *didn't* guess Vernona, Charlene, Stephanie and Kevin. You don't have to stop with name guessing. You can press your advantage by coyly wagering, "I'll bet there's a girl in your class who cries a lot."

"Hey, there is! There really is! Her name is Patty."

"And I'll bet there's a class meanie, too."

"How did *you* know? That's mostly why Patty cries. Because Peter hits her with the xylophone stick."

"And a class comedian—you know, someone that's always doing silly stuff?"

"Yeah, that's Howard. He always pours a cup of water on peoples' heads when they're taking a nap at rest time."

Now you have enough bits and scraps of intelligence to piece together the kind of Leading and Loaded Questions which your four-year-old will be unable to resist answering.

"When Peter hits *you* with the xylophone stick, do *you* cry?"

"Course not! I bop him with my tambourine!"

"When Howard pours water on *your* head at rest time, does it wake you up?"

"Well, the first day it did, but not anymore, because now before rest time I get a mouthful of water and don't swallow it, and then when Howard comes around I squirt him. That's what *all* the kids do."

Try not to be alarmed at what you may find out goes on behind the dotted swiss curtain. The important thing is not that Rhythm

Class is really a "bop" session, or that rest time is actually a continual water fight. The important thing is that your child does seem to be "making out."

COMFY OBJECT AT 40 MONTHS

18

Reasonably Good Housekeeping

The child who is encouraged to enter the mainstream of family life has a much better chance of realizing his or her potential than one who is not. But isn't encouraging a normally obstreperous youngster to "enter the mainstream of family life" likely to result in spotted rugs, marked-up baseboards, marred table tops and broken crockery? The answer, of course, is yes. But rugs can be cleaned, baseboards repainted, table tops revarnished and crockery replaced, while the damage to a youngster as a result of being made to feel

like a second-class member of the household may be irreparable. Or, to put it another way, it's far better to fulfill your responsibilities as a parent and let the house go to pot a little than to "keep things nice" and let your kid go to pot a lot.

Your job, then, is to keep the family home in reasonably good order, convincing Junior all the while that it's *his* castle, too. Some suggestions on the subject are offered in the following five-year guide to reasonably good housekeeping.

THE FIRST YEAR: THE FLOOR'S THE THING

During the hands-and-knees period, a child is necessarily floored. It's a mistake to try to protect your floor by restricting crawling activities to a couple of stain-proof rooms like the nursery and the kitchen. Your offspring should be given pretty much the crawl of the house. It you have a rug or rugs you're going to make a big fuss about when the inevitable happens, either convince yourself that they're only rugs, or take them up for the duration. No rug is worth giving a kid a complex over. Generally speaking, though, it's not so much a question of protecting the floor from Baby as it is a question of protecting Baby from the floor.

Your little crawler will do well enough on wood floors provided you watch out for splinters. Rugs, of course, are great for crawling,

as are asphalt, linoleum and plastic tile. One type of floor covering that is notably unsuitable for crawling is rush matting. If you don't believe us, just bare your knees and try crawling around on some for a while yourself.

It need hardly be said that Baby should be kept away from wiring. It should also go without saying that your floor must be kept clean enough to eat off, for Baby undoubtedly will—anything he or she can lift.

THE SECOND YEAR: CLEARING THE DECKS

About now, things begin to get really interesting. Baby, age one, has begun to walk, and it's clear that you are going to have to make some changes. Quick, better get those plants off that low table! And that lamp, put it up on the bookcase! Hurry, the kid's going after the milk glass! . . . But hold on a minute. This is turning into a shut-the-door-they're-coming-in-the-window affair. The situation calls for something better in the way of a solution than racing Baby to the milk glass. It's time for something like an agonizing reappraisal.

Are you really sold on your present decor? Aren't you a little sick of Cozy Cottage Colonial? And don't you think those wonderfully stark Shaker rooms that appeared in Architectural Digest last month were stunning? Well, even if you don't think so, you're probably beginning to get the idea. With your toddler up and about, you're going to have to clear the decks for action. Pretend that simplicity is the thing this year. Sell yourself on stark. Look what the Japanese can do with a hunk of bamboo and a few sheets of rice paper. Pretty

soon you won't be able to stand your pepper-mill lamp with its chintz-ruffed gingham shade. Fie, you will say, on your butter-churn umbrella stand. Milk glass you will eschew. Now, hurry, before you lose your nerve; gather up all these precious items and put them in a safe place. Of course, it's all just a maneuver. Down deep you love all your Cozy Cottage Colonial things as dearly as ever. You needn't feel the least bit guilty about relegating them to the attic. It's just a temporary measure. Our plan calls for their gradual reintroduction into the decor a few months hence.

Not only will your child have calmed down considerably by then, but he or she will have had an opportunity to learn to put that newfound walking ability to all sorts of wonderful uses—operating the pull-toy duck that says *quack* and the push-toy hen that says *cluck,* carrying armloads of toys around the house, jumping off the rug onto the floor, and just plain strutting—in short, much too busy to notice that the pepper-mill lamp has been sneaked back onto the drum table and that the butter-churn umbrella stand once again occupies its proud position by the door. As for that milk glass, it's probably a good idea to let it collect dust in the attic a little longer.

THE THIRD YEAR: TOY TROUBLE,
OR STUMBLING BLOCKS

During the third year the problem of toys begins to assume major proportions. The basic difficulty is easily pinpointed. A two-and-a-half-year-old is much better adapted to the job of dumping the contents of the toy box than a thirty-two-and-a-half-year-old Mommy is to the job of gathering them up and jamming them back into it. Pinpointing the solution to the problem, however, is not quite so easy. Getting sore won't help. The only way a child can find the yellow space gun is to dump the toy box and kick around through the rubble until it turns up. You certainly wouldn't want him to jeopardize that tender little gun hand by putting it into the toy box! There's not much point in getting sore at Daddy either, even though hardly a week passes that he doesn't add to the confusion with some new product of the toymaker's art.

You may as well face it: the tremendous accumulation of toys that is proving so prejudicial to reasonably good housekeeping isn't anybody's fault. It is just another result of "progress." Progress, never a simple thing to deal with, is especially diabolic in this case. But one thing is obvious—you're going to have to do *something*.

A good first step is to get rid of that big catchall toy box. It may have been a good idea back in the days when the baby's toy collection consisted of a half-dozen cuddly animals and a few rattles. It was really very handy, in an emergency, to be able to grab everything up and stuff it into the capacious toy box before the company arrived. But those days are long gone. It's been a good year since that capacious toy box held even half of the toys, the remaining half having been seeking its own level in such places as the bottom of the closet and beneath the junior bed.

Having put the old toy box out to pasture and dragged everything out of the closet and out from under the bed, you are faced with quite a pile. (Perhaps the toy box can be put out to pasture quite literally. With a coat of outside enamel, it may be just dandy to stand beside the sandbox as a wintering place for sand toys.)

Your general objective should be to give everything a sort of place. We say "sort of place" because there is an astronomical

number of items to store, and a strictly limited number of places in which to store them. Even if you were to cram your child's entire wardrobe into one drawer, that would still give you just a half-dozen or so empty drawers. Now cram the entire wardrobe into one drawer. Next, break the toys into as many groupings as you have empty drawers. All plastic Indians, cowboys, horses, cows and so on might make up one group; blocks, logs, bricks and so on, another; everything with wheels, another; musical instruments, another; and so forth. But since toys don't classify as neatly as flora and fauna, you're bound to end up with some arbitrary combinations. Don't let that worry you. The wind-up toys won't mind doubling up with the puzzles, nor will the yo-yos object to being thrown in with the educational toys. Then assign each group to a drawer. Drawers, of course, are most practical for much of the stuff that has to be stored, but any odd nooks, niches or crannies you can make available will certainly be useful, too. They're fine for stuffed animals. Your youngster might, in fact, object strenuously if you were to try to shut up that great and good friend Monkey in some stuffy old drawer.

The next thing to tackle is getting your child into the habit of putting things away. The worst mistake you can make at this point is to approach the subject head on. It's not fair to expect a two-and-a-half-year-old to do the job out of a sense of responsibility. Your objective should be simply to get the child used to the activity of putting things away. One fine day, after the new system has been in effect long enough that the child has become thoroughly familiar with it, you suffer a simulated lapse of memory.

"My goodness," you allow in your best casual tone, "I forget where these blocks go . . ."

"In here!" your child shrieks gleefully, scooping them up and putting them in the proper drawer—delighted with being the authority on where things go. "Not in dere!" he or she screams happily when you make "a mistake" and put a rhinoceros in the block drawer.

"My goodness!" you say, "how can you remember where all these things go? Now let me see, where do these sailboats go?"

"Here! Let me put 'em. You'll put 'em all wrong."

When your tot tires of playing the expert, you can enlarge your program to include a series of races and contests. A three-year-old can get pretty excited over such challenges as, "Let's see who can put away more bricks," and, "Can you put away all your crayons by the time Mommy finishes vacuuming the hall?" And if you conduct these dodges artfully enough, your child won't know till it's too late that it was all part of a devilish plot to train him or her to pick up the mess.

THE FOURTH YEAR:
THE HANDWRITING ON THE WOODWORK

There are some things you've just got to accept. For example, you may as well just accept the fact that your offspring is going to knock over about as much milk as he or she swallows, and compose your notes to the milkman accordingly. There's no use making your three-to-four-year-old cry over spilt milk. Though a good cry after a particularly wet day in the milk shed may do *you* a world of good.

In some areas, you have a choice. The crumb question, for instance, can be answered either way. It follows as the morning after the night before that if your child is at liberty to munch anywhere there is going to be a trail of crumbs from basement to attic. You can diminish the problem by avoiding such crumbly stuff as shortbread cookies, providing instead some such close-knit between-meal fare as pretzels, but you're still going to have to keep the vacuum handy even so. On the other hand, you don't *have* to put up with the crumbs at all. You can simply lay down a rule that all eating is to take place at the table. Bear in mind, though, that you are in somewhat the same position as the character in the fairy tale who was granted a quota of three wishes. Similarly, three rules is approximately your quota, so you'd better make each one count. If "No eating away from the table" is the sort of rule you can really put your heart into, by all means adopt it. But if it does not strike a really responsive chord, skip it and save the slot for a more important prohibition.

There are some kinds of behavior, however, that are entirely unacceptable, and must be sternly dealt with. It is usually during the fourth year that most children try their little hands at impromptu mural decoration. When you first discover the handwriting on the woodwork, your impulse, quite naturally, is to find the culprit and whale away. But would the punishment fit the crime? A review of what probably happened may help you decide. Let's see, now. Little Angelica was watching "Captain Wallabey," and The Captain was explaining about rectangles. He showed how a rectangle was like a long square, and how you could draw a whole picture using just rectangles, with a rectangle house and a rectangle sun and rectangle tree. Pretty interesting stuff. But as he eases into the commercial: *"Oh,* look! What have we here! *Yes!* It's a box! A box of *Flakies!* And what *sha-ape* is the box? . . . That-a-at's right! It's a *rec-tangle* . . ." Little Angelica eases out from in front of the set and rolls over near the sofa. What's that under the sofa? A crayon. An *orange* crayon! She thinks that if she had a piece of paper she'd draw a rectangle. There's paper in her room. But the nice white baseboard is right there by the tip of the crayon, and if she moves the crayon just *that* much . . . What you have on your hands, it would seem, is not a "crime" at all, but a normal, experimentally minded three-and-a-half-year-old with a healthy resistance to sneaky commercials. But, you may protest, isn't a three-and-a-half-year-old *old* enough to know better than to write on the wood-

work? No, not at all. There are very few things in life that any of us "know" simply by virtue of having reached a certain age. The child is, however, old enough to be *taught* better than to write on the woodwork.

Of course, he or she has to learn that it's wrong to deface the household. But it's even more important that a child learn *why* it's wrong. If you can begin to give a real understanding of what it means to be a member of the household, the life expectancy of the old homestead may be appreciably extended. You can't expect to get very far toward accomplishing this goal unless you address your little miscreant in terms he or she can understand.

Parents have often been warned not to "talk down" to their child. Presenting new ideas in terms a child is most likely to understand is not "talking down." It's just common sense. An utterly irrelevant explanation of why it's not a good idea to write on the woodwork in terms of how hard all those nice builders had to work to build our nice house for us is likely to mean a lot more to a child than an utterly relevant one on the same subject in terms of how hard *Daddy* had to work to make enough money to *pay* all those nice builders. An explanation in terms of some immediate experience is likely to be especially effective. "Remember a couple of days ago when we painted your steam shovel and dump truck?" He nods enthusiastically. "Well, suppose somebody came along and put crayon marks all over the nice new paint. How would you like that?"

He glowers ferociously. "I'd sock him!" he states with heat.

"Well, you might not. You might just want to explain to him that you're not supposed to write on toys. And then he'd want to help you clean them up!"

"I'd get a big stick and sock him over the head!"

"Now, here's some cleanser, and here's a rag for you and a rag for me."

"I'd—I'd push him in the mud!"

"There! That's fine! Now it's all bright and clean again. Say, where are you going?"

"I gotta go out and look at my steam shovel and dump truck."

THE FIFTH YEAR: THE BIG PICKUP

Baby has finally made kindergarten, and you have your long-awaited opportunity for a really full-dress expedition into the breeding ground of most of your housekeeping troubles—Baby's bedroom. Up to now you have been restricted to the risky business of a commando raid every now and then—a quick dash into the room while your tot was out bike riding, an armful of tangled toys grabbed from under the bed, and a quick dash to the cellar, where they were thrust into the utility closet with the booty of previous raids. You recall with a chill that dreadful time he or she came home unexpectedly from Debby's and caught you red-handed. But you're through with all that. The kid's a mile away at kindergarten, and won't be home till the school bus arrives.

As you stand there with your mop and your broom and your big wire trash burner, looking slowly around your child's room, you feel, for a minute, as Pip in *Great Expectations* must have felt when he first entered Miss Havisham's sitting room. An icy draft of panic stabs through you. You want to run. We'll board it up, you think wildly, and start over from scratch in the guest room! But the awful

feeling passes and you come to your senses. It's not so bad, you think, recalling that you've already made a start. The many and varied collections were prime difficulties, and some weeks ago you convinced your offspring that the professional thing to do was to *catalog* them. With your help the stone collection, the feather collection, the bottle-top collection, the tooth collection, shell collection, Dixie-lid collection and *all* the other collections were transferred from the ragtag assortment of boxes which had housed them to a set of kitchen cannisters which you contributed to the project. You think with a sense of profound relief that never again will you wonder what's in that old Whitman's Sampler box, and idly lift the lid to find six grubby, grisly cicada shells staring eyelessly up at you.

When attacking a problem as far gone as a child's room, it's important to treat the causes rather than symptoms. The dust, the

cobwebs and the general disorder are all symptoms. The cause of the trouble is that there is just about twice as much stuff in the room as there should be. The solution is plain. Half the stuff must go. But eliminating half of your child's goods willy-nilly is certainly not the answer. The trick is to perform the feat in such a way that the child never feels victimized. This is not the impossible stunt it may seem. The secret to bringing it off is the fact that a child hardly, if ever, uses half the things in the room. It is simply a matter, then, of clearing out the half that is hardly, if ever, used. There are three techniques which are basic to the task. These are Thinning, Platooning and Stashing.

"Thinning" involves the permanent withdrawal of an item from circulation. This has nothing to do with the elimination of broken toys, torn books and the like, but refers specifically to items that are as good as the day they were received from Uncle Ned, Aunt Ellen and Cousin John. Generally speaking, toys that are considered more trouble than they are worth are good candidates for thinning.

After double-checking to see that you have not thinned anything that the youngster is likely to miss, stow your haul in the top of the storage closet. Next to the tree lights is a good place. Then it will

automatically turn up when you need presents for Uncle Ned's, Aunt Ellen's and Cousin John's kids.

"Platooning" is the short-term withdrawal of groups of toys on a circulating basis. For example, your child has about seven dozen records in the collection. Since he or she is interested in only about a dozen at a time, you may as well get the remaining six dozen out of the way. As the records in play begin to tire, they can be taken out and a fresh platoon sent in.

In addition to being useful in cleaning out the room, platooning is helpful in other ways. It is a great help, in times of crisis—during a seige of measles, for example—to be able to trot out great numbers of toys which your child has all but forgotten. Almost any type of toy can be platooned. It's just a question of what you can get away with.

"Stashing" involves the storing of items that are unsuitable, owing to your tot's tender age, until he or she is old enough at least to read the directions.

Gigantic construction kits containing everything you need to make an authentic scale model of the *U.S.S. Missouri* are eminently stashable. So are magic sets, puzzle sets, electrical toys, microscope outfits, chemistry sets and giant 1,000-piece fun-for-the-whole-family jigsaw puzzles. The duration of the stashing period varies with the item. The Mighty Mo construction kit can be brought out just as soon as Junior is old enough to understand that it must not be taken into the tub when Daddy finally gets it finished, while that 1,000-piece jigsaw puzzle, on the other hand, should be stashed practically indefinitely.

But you can't expect to bring order out of chaos in one morning. You'd better start tapering off; that school bus will be pulling up at any minute now.

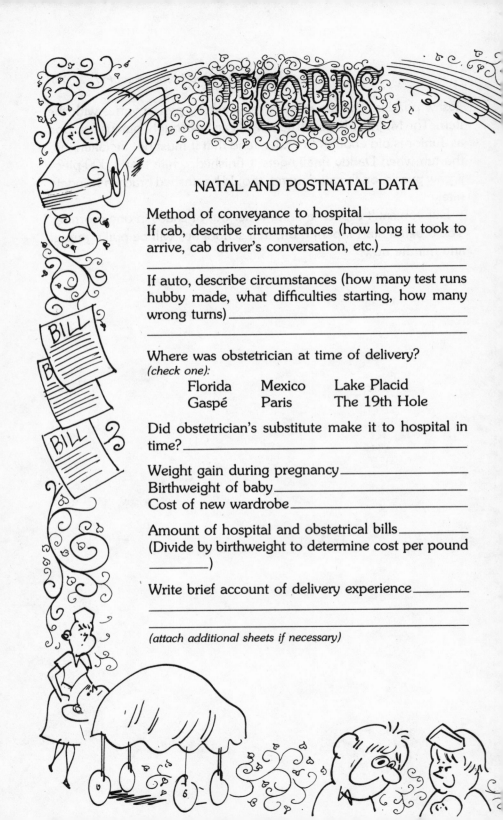

RECORDS

NATAL AND POSTNATAL DATA

Method of conveyance to hospital_____

If cab, describe circumstances (how long it took to arrive, cab driver's conversation, etc.) _____
_____

If auto, describe circumstances (how many test runs hubby made, what difficulties starting, how many wrong turns) _____
_____

Where was obstetrician at time of delivery?
(check one):

Florida	Mexico	Lake Placid
Gaspé	Paris	The 19th Hole

Did obstetrician's substitute make it to hospital in time?_____

Weight gain during pregnancy_____
Birthweight of baby_____
Cost of new wardrobe_____

Amount of hospital and obstetrical bills_____
(Divide by birthweight to determine cost per pound _____)

Write brief account of delivery experience_____
_____
_____

(attach additional sheets if necessary)

Number of calls from diaper services, photographers, insurance men, day camps, nursery schools, etc., during first day at home_____

First argument over frequency of visits from maternal grandmother

_____   _____   _____
date   *duration*   *intensity*

First toy purchased for Baby by Baby's daddy
(check one)

Doll   Rocking horse
Electric trains   Erector set
Catcher's mitt   Ice skates
Sled   Tea set

First kept parents awake all night_____
                                                        (date)

Names of people who were sent announcements but who did not send presents

_____,   _____,   _____,

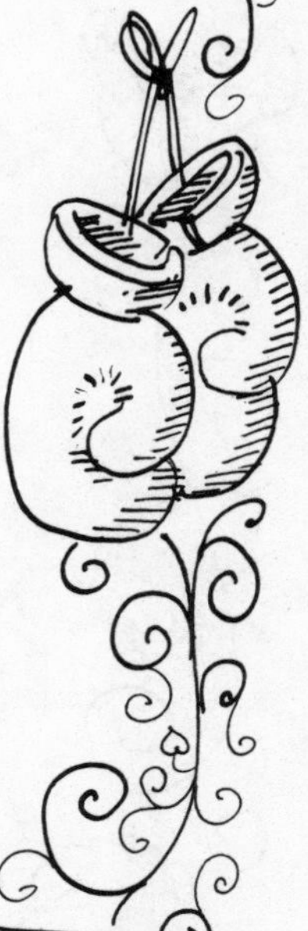

_____,   _____,   _____,

Application made to college of choice_____
                                                             (date)

Whom does Baby look like?
(state whose)

_____ eyes,   _____ ears,
_____ nose,   _____ hair,
_____ chin,   _____ coloring,
_____ dimples.

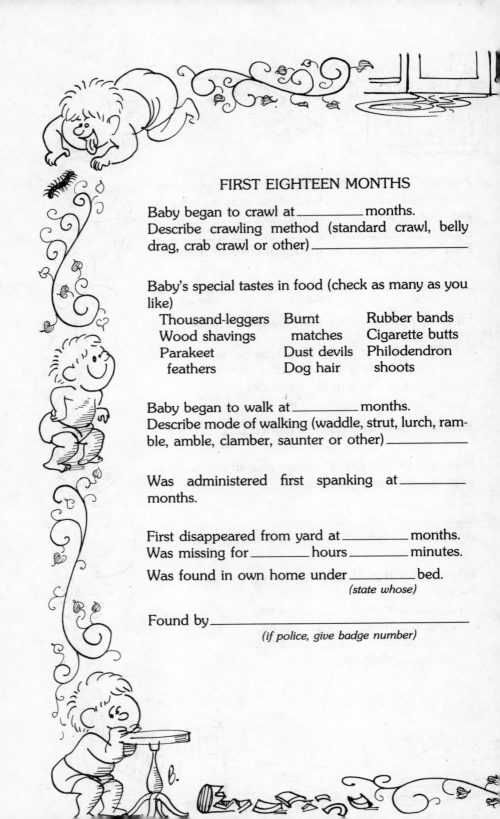

FIRST EIGHTEEN MONTHS

Baby began to crawl at _____ months.
Describe crawling method (standard crawl, belly drag, crab crawl or other) _____

Baby's special tastes in food (check as many as you like)

Thousand-leggers   Burnt   Rubber bands
Wood shavings   matches   Cigarette butts
Parakeet   Dust devils   Philodendron
   feathers   Dog hair   shoots

Baby began to walk at _____ months.
Describe mode of walking (waddle, strut, lurch, ramble, amble, clamber, saunter or other) _____

Was administered first spanking at _____ months.

First disappeared from yard at _____ months.
Was missing for _____ hours _____ minutes.
Was found in own home under _____ bed.
(state whose)

Found by _____
(if police, give badge number)

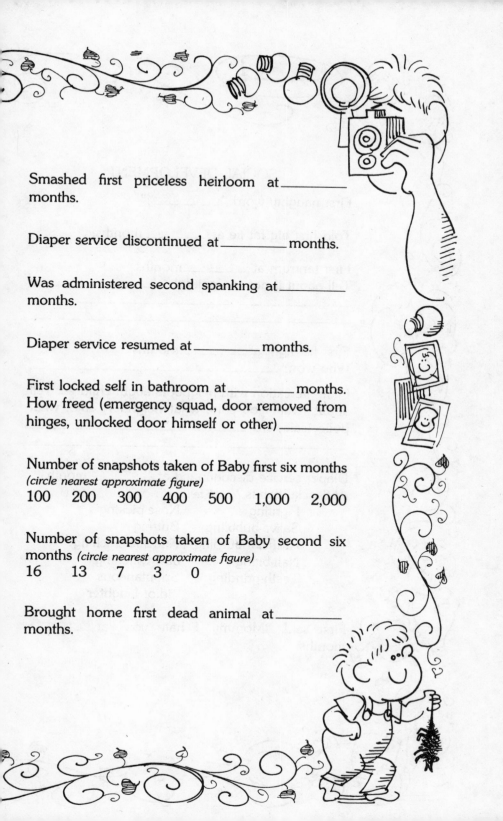

Smashed first priceless heirloom at_____ months.

Diaper service discontinued at_____ months.

Was administered second spanking at_____ months.

Diaper service resumed at_____ months.

First locked self in bathroom at_____ months. How freed (emergency squad, door removed from hinges, unlocked door himself or other)_____

Number of snapshots taken of Baby first six months
(circle nearest approximate figure)
100   200   300   400   500   1,000   2,000

Number of snapshots taken of Baby second six months *(circle nearest approximate figure)*
16   13   7   3   0

Brought home first dead animal at_____ months.

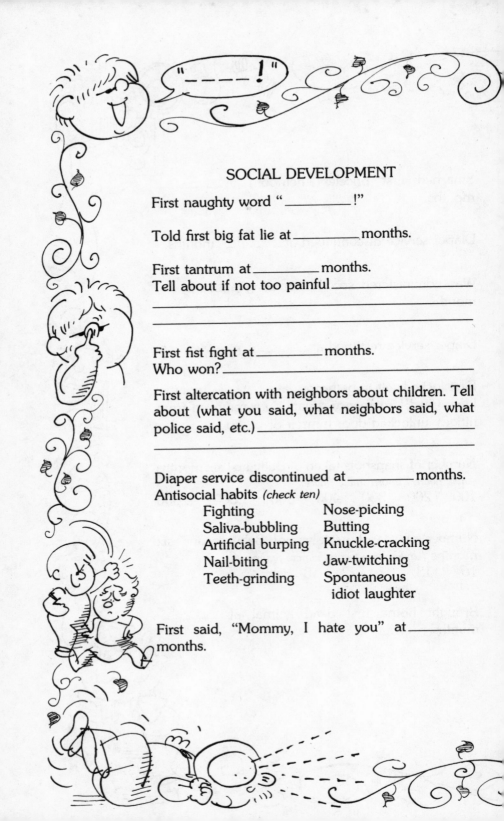

SOCIAL DEVELOPMENT

First naughty word "_____!"

Told first big fat lie at _____ months.

First tantrum at _____ months.
Tell about if not too painful _____
_____
_____

First fist fight at _____ months.
Who won? _____

First altercation with neighbors about children. Tell about (what you said, what neighbors said, what police said, etc.) _____
_____

Diaper service discontinued at _____ months.
Antisocial habits *(check ten)*

    Fighting   Nose-picking
    Saliva-bubbling   Butting
    Artificial burping   Knuckle-cracking
    Nail-biting   Jaw-twitching
    Teeth-grinding   Spontaneous
                      idiot laughter

First said, "Mommy, I hate you" at _____ months.

Punched first sitter at _____ months.

Diaper service resumed at _____ months.

First birthday party
(circle word or phrase that most nearly characterizes party)

Fiasco	Total failure
Never again	Calamity
Washout	Nobody was
Holocaust	actually killed
Disaster	

First said, "Hello, stupid" to perfect stranger at ____
_____ months.

Favorite insults

_____, _____, _____,
_____, _____, _____,

First cheated at a game at _____ months.

Brought home first awful joke at _____ months.
Give tag line_____

Decided that "BM" was the funniest word in the
language at _____ months.